THE
COMING
CHRIST

THE COMING CHRIST

A REVELANT
AND TIMELY
STUDY OF
BIBLE PROPHECY
CONCERNING
THE END TIMES
AND JESUS'
SECOND COMING

Tom Buttram

Gospel Tract Society
Independence, MO

www.gospeltractsociety.org

First printing: Febraury 2012

ISBN: 978-1-4675-1795-9

Design: Ted Ferguson

Printed in the United States of America

Please visit our websites for other great articles and information:
www.thecomingchrist.com
www.gospeltractsociety.org

For information regarding publicity for author interviews contact
Tom Buttram at (816)461-6086

Special thanks are acknowledged to my sister-in-law, Beth Buttram, and my nephew, David Paul Buttram for their helpful editing and continual collaboration.

Gratitude is expressed for the faithfulness of my parents, Lester and Ethel Buttram, who devoted their lives to the lost and needy. Their generosity and sacrifice blessed all who knew or met them. It goes without saying, but won't: that I felt the strong call of God to speak the truth of His Word concerning the times that are to come.

The illumination of The Holy Spirit, concerning the elements in this book, bowled us over, while we were in the very process of writing these pages—as things we had never seen before, came so clear.

CONTENTS

INTRODUCTION

We are glad to share this work with you, but by no means do we expect this to answer all the questions you may have concerning the end of days, or cover all the subjects that intermingle with each other, as Scripture tends to sometimes ask more questions than it answers. We have seen many time lines that attempt to explain the order of end-time events, but if those lines are thorough to Scripture, they are too dense to understand. That is because there is a lot going on from today until the time that the New Heaven and Earth come down.

Using Aircraft Analogies for the Hard Points

This writer has an interest in aircraft and flying, thus, often an analogy from aviation will be used to further our understanding, and right now is a good time for one of those analogies.

A friend of mine is an aircraft designer. He is the most prolific producer of WWI aircraft reproduction kits in the world. He designed and built all the planes used in the movie, *"Fly Boys."* When sitting with him at his computer trying to design an airframe that will look a certain way and handle a certain way, Rob shows me where the "hard points" must be established. Then, everything else simply flows from that envelope of design.

A "hard point" is where the strength of the aircraft is focused—as in where you attach the wings, wing struts, engine, and landing gear. Where those things bolt on to the airframe, there must be inherent (designed in advance) strength and stability, because if either of those components fail, you most likely will make the evening news.

 Identifying the Hard Points

After the hard points are established, gauges, accessories, and minor control surfaces (such as trim), can be easily and conveniently placed. As you read the following pages, our goal is that you will be able to identify and properly place the "hard points" of prophetic Scriptures.

An example of one hard point is this: "...a time of trouble, such as never was since there was a nation even to that same time." When you see this description of such a time, even though the words may vary a bit, you can be assured that this is a "hard point." You will see it in several different places, but it is the same thing, and NOT several separate times. This particular hard point describes the Great Tribulation, and the length of it is given in different places as 3 ½ years, or 42 months, or 1260 days. Still today, so many people want to bolt the wing to a point called seven years. There is a hard point called "Seven Years," but that's not where you bolt the wing, because something else goes there. So that our "prophecy craft" flies, we have to correctly identify a seven-year event.

As people design their own "prophecy craft," many follow the failed plans of predecessors who didn't learn about hard points, and just bolt major components where they are aesthetically pleasing, but mostly because they are in the habit of doing what they are told to believe. Seeing abandoned prophecy craft projects in every backyard is what prompted this book. People give up their work before it is completed, because as it nears completion, there are a lot of pieces that don't fit and it seems hopeless to understand, and burn-out takes them over.

From my observation, the hard points that must be identified, in order for safe flight to be accomplished, are:
1. The timing of the In-Gathering/Resurrection.
2. The length of the Great Tribulation.
3. The meaning and timing of God's Wrath.
4. The meaning of "at the last trump."
5. The meaning and time of "Judgment."
6. The definition of "create" and "destroy."
7. First-fruits, general Harvest, and Gleanings, of the First Resurrection
8. The Second Resurrection of the dead.

These eight items are distinct in nature, one from the other, and having them properly placed is vital.

Future, Present, and Past Tense
When we study any subject in the Bible, we find that many times there is no chronological order of events, except when they are mentioned in the same sentence or setting. The difficulty, for example, is understanding the Book of Revelation. There, the same event is referred to in several different settings. First in introduction as future tense, then in present-future tense, and even past-future tense. That is often a stumbling block for many, because as tenses change, we still have

to remember that it is from "Day Vision" awareness that John is speaking from. Evidently, he wrote from his memory of a God-ordained vision and of the things he saw, and recording them on paper must have been a task past man's ability. We can understand, though, with study from other prophets like Daniel, Joel, Isaiah, and Ezekiel. Our attempt to provide clarity to the subject of the Resurrection, by studying one event at a time, proved to be an impossibility, as these events explain themselves by relationship to each other. So, as you have it in the Bible, you will see it here, and hopefully, it will come together and become a comfort to you.

Chapter 1

GROUND SCHOOL

Every child must at some time have had the experience of holding his or her hand flat, like an airplane wing, out the car window, and feeling the power of the moving air raise or lower their hand like an airplane going up or down. That is a certain amount of experience, but not enough to learn how to fly. Every pilot must learn the principles of flight. First of all, we learn *"Bernoulli's Principle,"*

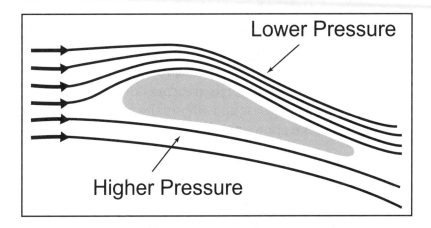

Lower Pressure

Higher Pressure

which explains how an airfoil shaped like a bird's wing gives lift when air passes over it. Then, the mechanics and science of air density, weather, aircraft, and human nature (so we understand why we make decisions), eventually come together so actual flight instruction can begin. It is vital to the pilot, so that the number of his landings are always equal to the number of his take-offs, that he understands proven principles of flight and laws of mechanics and nature—so that when decisions must be made, the response can be trusted.

Understanding Things to Come

That is where we are just prior to the study of prophetic Scripture, which will lead us to a much greater and comforting understanding of the things to come. We cannot simply hop in an airplane or helicopter without prior knowledge of weight and balance or thrust and drag, just as we can't study the end of time without an understanding of the beginning of time; the Heaven to come without knowing the Heaven before. However, while we could spend hundreds of pages on these preparatory subjects and become satiated (filled and satisfied) before the steak is served or simply fatigued, we will just offer Biblically sound glimpses of the "Big Picture," footnoting Scripture occasionally, so we can understand, for instance, the nature of the Antichrist and the purpose of the Great Tribulation that will mark the end of days. Certainly not—that we are looking for the Antichrist, but for the signs that precede the end of times and the Coming of Christ, [1] so that we, each of us, become preachers of Truth—not fiction—and thereby possess and offer to the seeker the Gospel of Jesus Christ in its pure form.[2]

Speaking With Truth and Clarity

Perhaps one of the saddest phenomena of the subject of Christ's Return and the importance of Truth concerning the subject, is ambivalence of it by the Body of Christ, the Church. So few people feel the need to know the nature of all aspects of the Lord's Return, because they have been taught that it has little consequence to them. Many Christians have been taught and believe with certainty that they will be excused from the trials and testing of the Great Tribulation. They somehow aren't aware that Christianity is and has been hated by this world, and that those who carry the name of Christ have been martyred and oppressed since Day One, A.D. The reason, for example, that the Jews have had a contract on their lives, ever since there was a Jew, is because Satan is the enemy of God. He hates the Chosen Ones, whether they be of Israel's descent, or they be the offspring of her seed (Christians).[3]

Because the ambivalent Christians of today have attached "God's Wrath" to an incorrect, unreinforced, or soft point location on the airframe and it keeps working loose, they just moan, "It's just beyond me," and walk off, wishing not to talk about it to anyone. Today, you and I together, can speak with Truth and authority about the times and events to come, simply by reading the instructions over until clarity comes. We will carefully attach to the hard points those things that fit. Once we get one thing bolted in place, then other pieces fit by default.

While this isn't a book to tell people how to think and interpret the Bible Scriptures, it is a guide with the purpose to expose erroneous teachings that have rendered the Church deceived and powerless, whereas the power we should possess as God's Children to disciple all nations has been exchanged for a weak presentation of the Gospel, and a congregation of churchgoers who are playing "follow the leader." Perhaps it will cause the reader to ferret out nuggets of Truth, little by little, until the puzzle of understanding is complete.

THE BIG PICTURE

For many people, the greatest pitfall to faith in God is the picture of Creation—taken from the Bible. Then we set that against facts from Earth Science and astronomy, coupled with a wild notion of evolution in an attempt to bridge those facts of history and our being on the earth physically, to form a God-less concept of "How Did All This Happen?"

On the surface, and according to the manner in which the Genesis account of Creation is taught to us, earth's history, and the presence of this amazing universe, seem to be at odds with each other. Many Christians blindly accept the six-thousand-year-old-earth story, and on good basis. Non-believers accept evidence of fossils, geo-stratum, and other "clocks" that set the existence of earth, our solar system, and the universe much, much longer—and with good reason.

The Theory of Evolution – Just a Theory!
Since the assumed ancient age of the earth is much longer than what seems to be given as the Biblical account in the Book of Genesis, another method that explains the existence of life needed to come forth, thus—Darwin's Theory of Evolution! The only thing that evolution proves, is that God used

His creative nature to baffle His Creation, by filling each created life-form with mystery, brilliance, and beauty. To make nature more intriguing, He made both male and female at the same time so the story continues, generation after generation.

It is pretty easy to discount the theory of evolution, by going no further than its title — *it's just a theory,* and one truly believed by only a few scientists. For others who are not the "true believers" of evolution, they only purport to believe it in order to maintain their standing in the science or academic community, and because—there seems to be no other explanation, as Creation itself, seems too unbelievable to come from another intelligent source than ourselves.

Finding the Answer in Genesis
The answer to the distance spanned by the Creation account and a very, very old universe, including the earth, may well be found in the first five verses of the Bible:

1.) In the beginning God created the heaven and the earth.
2.) And the earth was without form, and void; and darkness was upon the face of the deep. And the Spirit of God moved upon the face of the waters.
3.) And God said, Let there be light: and there was light.
4.) And God saw the light, that it was good: and God divided the light from the darkness.
5.) And God called the light Day, and the darkness he called Night. And the evening and the morning were the first day.

I have heard preachers and teachers try to explain this event for decades. By studying the first five verses, we can quickly understand much of what has baffled men for centuries. *"In the beginning"* implies that "at the very first of things," God created heaven and earth. It certainly is not clear that He created the two places (heaven and earth) as separate things, though most of us would assume that to be the case. However, heaven and earth could very well be the same place, but in different atomic phases, one being spiritual, the other physical—consisting of atom building-blocks.

The Key of Understanding

Moving to verse two, we find the key of understanding between a very young earth and an ancient earth in an ancient universe. Before "days" were such a thing, the earth was already present—and for a long time—perhaps eternity. It was dark, without form (mountains, valleys, trees, plateaus, rivers, etc.), or beauty, and void of landmarks. Darkness was upon the deep and waters covered the face of most of it. Up to this point, Time had no purpose, no limits. After all, without the rotation of the earth within its orbit around the Sun, there is no concept of day or night—nothing to set a clock to. At that point, Time was: Now, Existence Past, and Existence to Come.

For example, Astronauts in outer space have no concept of Time because the Sun is always bright and shining. Without Cape Kennedy calling to tell them when to go to bed and when to wake up, they would get quite confused.

Though the earth was in existence in the formless, dark, wet void, it possibly had no life as we know it, or had different life forms. Most likely, it was cold, very cold, cold enough for an Ice Age lasting a long time. Until verse three, Time did not exist, but the earth did exist—and for a very long time.

The Earth is Full of Elements

Before we look at verse three, it is profitable to go back to our high school science class and review the *"Periodic Table of Elements."* The only thing to gather from it right now, is the definition of an "element." An element is any pure matter that cannot be further reduced. It can neither be destroyed, nor created. That's why, in the Middle Ages, "alchemists" were treated as witches, or worse, for trying to create gold and silver. These and other elements belong to God as His Creation and cannot be duplicated. The earth is full of elements, and in a larger sense, might itself be considered an element of sorts, since it can't be created or destroyed. I might lose you here with that statement, because you are aware that God created the earth and one day the Lord said that He will destroy the earth by fire! Well, that is the next point I need to make in order to understand the Big Picture. I think this is the moment we need to seize upon, so we can understand God's use of "Create" and "Destroy."

The True Meaning of "Create" and "Destroy"
A football team coming off the home field with a humiliating loss of 98 to 3 is described by the sportscasters as a team **"destroyed"** on their home field. The look on their faces is that of absolute humiliation. The same for a boxer who was unprepared for the big fight; headlines read: "Whitney **destroyed** by a barrage of upper cuts and left hooks—in the third round."

In Genesis 9:11, God covenanted with Noah, that *"...neither shall there any more be a flood to destroy the earth."* "Destroy," as God uses it here, evidently doesn't mean what we think destroy literally means—"obliterate into nonexistence," but more like what we use in general conversation, to "take down a notch or two," "rearrange," or "recycle."

Likewise, the term "Create" must have the same meaning. For example: gold cannot be created or destroyed. A beautiful gold ring can, however, be "created," in that, by rearranging its structure, it takes on new form and function. Dropping it into a running gear box can "destroy" the ring by ruining its form and function, though it is still a ring. Sending that same ring back to the jeweler to be recreated, perhaps to even a more stylish design, is what seems to happen to the earth, during the different "earths" or ages it passes through. It is "created" to its new form and function, and magnificently too, as it is destroyed almost beyond recognition.

God Creates Light

In verse three, God brought light upon the earth by calling it into existence. However that happened, it was a very large miracle. Did He bring a star from a distant galaxy, destined for this moment, or did He ignite a nuclear fuel mass in this dark solar system with the power of His voice? Perhaps He removed a particle curtain that filtered the light that was already there. We can only speculate.

Dividing the Light and Darkness

Verse four might reflect the orbits and rotations in which He placed the planets and moons, to divide the light and darkness...

"And God called the light Day, and the darkness he called Night." And that was the first day—when time began. God is the Creator and He has always created; furthermore, He will continue to create, though we think of Creation as being a one-time event.

In the beginning, God created the heaven and earth; there were new earths to follow and new Heavens as well, in the thinking of Creation being something new, reflecting a different form and function. God will also destroy the earth again, in the thinking of "trashing" it before creating it again.

Two Destructions Yet to Come

It appears that two destructions are yet to come:

1. The one at Christ's Second Coming when graves are opened and great earthquakes, including God's Wrath, will "destroy" much of the earth's form and function, but the most notable change will be the removal of the curse placed on the earth at the onset of sin. Returning the earth to its pre-curse condition is one of the things that will give man the promised 1,000 years. That, and a very great earthquake that levels the mountains and causes the islands to disappear will cause the death of all who remain on the earth.

2. The destruction by fire at the end of Christ's Millennial (thousand year) reign on earth, (3,000 A.D. approx.) will be the final earth destruction. At that time, fire destroys all the works of man with molten fire, then the earth is recreated in the form of the original Garden of Eden. That happens before the Father creates and brings down the new Heaven and Earth[1] (as one unit), and He does so for the final time. Now, the planet Earth is already there, so what He brings down is the "preparation" and conclusion that will enthrone Him in the presence of those who chose to love and worship Him for eternity. There is another thing that is destroyed by the "destruction by fire"—Choice. The thing that made choice possible, the Law of Opposition, is now at this point—deactivated. It still exists, but in a remote sense, as the poles of moral expression are separated by the seal on the Pit of Hell.

It will be a perfect Creation for those who love Him to spend eternity worshiping Him and basking in the Light of His Presence and Glory.[2] It will be a very physical world, not invisible as we have been taught, and it will contain pleasure of the senses past our imagination.[3] Best of all, as in the Garden of Eden, the taint and perversion by sin will be absent.

Our bodies will be glorified "Creations," because God will take us as we are now and place the intended perfect design of Eden upon us, by Glorification.

A Wonderful Change
This essay by Henry Morris gives us pause to consider the wonderful change coming to those who are faithful and who overcome sin.

Our Glorious Bodies

"We look for the Saviour, the Lord Jesus Christ: Who shall change our vile body, that it may be fashioned like unto his glorious body, according to the working whereby he is able even to subdue all things unto himself" (Philippians 3:20-21).

Two vivid contrasts are highlighted in this text: We now have a vile body that will be changed into a glorious body. Our Lord Jesus will fashion us after the pattern of His own body.

There is ample evidence, both in Scripture and in our own experience, that our present physical bodies are "vile." The English word seems more intense than the Greek, which simply means "lowly" or "humble." Christ humbled himself when he took on our flesh (Philippians 2:8). The Virgin Mary saw herself in a "low estate" as she compared herself to the wonder of what was happening to her (Luke 1:48).

But one glorious day, the Lord Jesus will change our humble bodies into that which is reflective of His own. *"Beloved, now are we the sons of God, and it doth not yet appear what we shall be: but we know that, when he shall appear, we shall be like him; for we shall see him as he is"* (1 John 3:2). What a marvelous thought! Even *"after my skin worms destroy this body, yet in my flesh shall I see God"* (Job 19:26).

The exciting description of those absolute changes are encapsulated in 1 Corinthians 15:42-58. We have a mortal body now, but then it will be imperishable. There is no honor to our bodies now, but then they will be glorious. Weakness is our burden now, but in eternity we will be endued with power. Thank You, Heavenly Father, for this majestic promise. HMM III

Chapter 3

THE SEVEN EARTHS

In partial summary of Creation, it seems that as we understand Creation (not being made from scratch, but being reassembled from existing components), there is not just one earth in the Bible, but seven. The planet of Earth is one, but the re-creations of redesigned earths are seven. They are:

1. The original earth, dark, and without form or function. It was created "in the beginning."

2. The new earth, created in six days, with day and night, dry land with form, separated by seas. A beautiful land of Eden for Adam and Eve.

3. The earth of God's perfection, now marred by sin, is cursed so the ground does not not bear food without man's labor and toil. The lush garden paradise is now a desert with pests, decay, pain, and death. God's perfection, now violated by the curse of sin.

4. The earth destroyed by the Great Flood. Antediluvian (never rained) atmosphere exchanged for periods of flood and drought; atmosphere loses vapor solar shield, causing cancer; atmospheric pressure drops 60%, leaving us in an

oxygen deprivation situation, thus man's days decrease from 900 years to 120 years. In addition, the continents break up, forming island chains and separate land masses, and the earth heaps up mountains and leaves great valleys. Loss of density altitude brings extinction to the animals and plants of great size—those needing intense oxygen to breathe. Violent weather outbursts are now the norm.

5. The earth suffers another destruction just preceding and following the Second Coming of Christ; fire falls from the heavens, massive earthquakes, and wide scale destruction renders the earth a very hostile place to live.

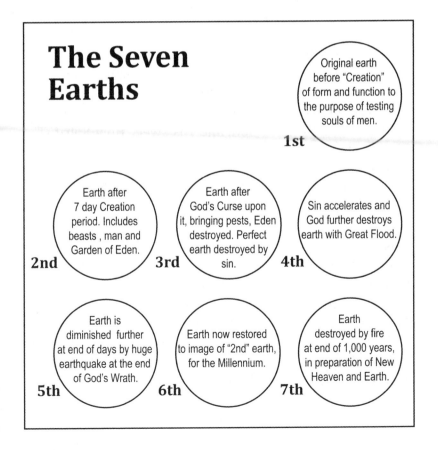

The Seven Earths

1st — Original earth before "Creation" of form and function to the purpose of testing souls of men.

2nd — Earth after 7 day Creation period. Includes beasts, man and Garden of Eden.

3rd — Earth after God's Curse upon it, bringing pests, Eden destroyed. Perfect earth destroyed by sin.

4th — Sin accelerates and God further destroys earth with Great Flood.

5th — Earth is diminished further at end of days by huge earthquake at the end of God's Wrath.

6th — Earth now restored to image of "2nd" earth, for the Millennium.

7th — Earth destroyed by fire at end of 1,000 years, in preparation of New Heaven and Earth.

6. Following God's Wrath upon those bearing the Mark of the Beast that comes after the Great Tribulation, the earth is "created" to a restored earth like the second earth. Evidently, even the heavy oxygen-rich atmosphere (resembling a giant hyperbaric chamber) will be restored; as the time lived on earth by God's saints, and those born into that earth[1], will be a thousand years.[2]

7. Just like the days of the week, the seventh earth represents completion. This earth will be the Sabbath of Creation. It comes after the last testing by Satan, the war Satan attempts against God, and the Judgment Seat of Christ. At that time, the earth will burn with a great fervent fire and all the works of man will be destroyed.

The final creation of the earth comes shortly after the final destruction, as the new Heaven and Earth come down. Heaven will be a cubic city, 1500 miles north and south, east and west, and straight up. God the Father will reside there, as well as the Lamb of God, and His sweet Holy Spirit. The river of life will flow from the Throne of God, and trees will grow on either side of the river, bearing different fruit each month, and the leaves of those trees will provide healing for the nations.[3]

This light study of the first five verses of the Bible already shows us how contradictions and misguided teachings can affect our understanding of Heaven and Earth, of Creation, and Destruction. Imagine how different the outcome of today's world might be if we were able to read God's Word with understanding, then we would be more accepting of God's story of Creation and the Creator, and less apt to follow some perverted "theory of evolution."

4

THE (RE)CREATION OF HEAVEN

The first five verses we previously read in Genesis showed us the heaven and the earth in place before God (re) created them in their new "form and function." You'll notice that until now they were not named, or "christened," until God gave them the names they have now, certainly indicating their newness.

The next five verses go into a general description of Heaven's Creation. Because many Bible students cannot accept the concept of Heaven and Earth as being one, they go off on tangents by saying the "firmament" has another "celestial" meaning such as outer space, thereby altering the foundation of everything we read in the following books of the Bible. It is impossible for us to define the boundaries of Heaven or even the center where the Throne now sits. We don't have to; we just need to understand that Heaven is where God is and where He operates His Glory out of.

Jewish belief teaches from the Torah, a Biblical understanding of "Seven Heavens," three of which reflect habitation.

Strangely, other major religions such as Hinduism, and Islam, also teach an existence of seven heavens, reflecting the perfection of God's use of the number seven, even among false religions. Most surely, our conventional concept of Heaven is not Biblical, and it is certainly not a place where most people actually anticipate with determined desire (sitting on a cloud, strumming on a harp).

God Creates the Firmament

6.) And God said, Let there be a firmament in the midst of the waters, and let it divide the waters from the waters.

7.) And God made the firmament, and divided the waters which were under the firmament from the waters which were above the firmament: and it was so.

8.) And God called the firmament Heaven. And the evening and the morning were the second day.

9.) And God said, Let the waters under the heaven be gathered together unto one place, and let the dry land appear: and it was so.

10.) And God called the dry land Earth; and the gathering together of the waters called he Seas: and God saw that it was good.

In verses 8 and 10, we witness the naming of Heaven, Earth, and the Seas. These are proper names as shown by capitalization, whereas when used before, heaven and earth were referred to as "raw material," and not recognized for the special purpose which was to come, and which deserve special recognition. The noun, "heaven," is also a general term for the cosmos, or heavenlies, which includes everything outside the earth.

Most amazing about what happens in verse eight, is that God called the firmament "HEAVEN," with a capital H! The firmament is what He divided the Seas with. The firmament also divided the waters above the firmament from the waters below the firmament. This explanation is so clear that most then must insist that firmament means something else.

The first part of the Big Picture, that of Creation of the physical Earth and Heaven, is the foundation of the second part and that of the special purpose: Why are we here?

Chapter 5

WHY ARE WE HERE?

I t is honest, sincere fellowship that the Lord of Heaven desired, but didn't have in the former or first Heaven. Angels and beasts of worship praised and worshiped God, because they were designed and created to do so. Even a rock gives glory to God, doing what rocks do: they stay put, stay together, anchor things, absorb and give off heat, and in their own way—they are beauteous.

Each of us may receive recognition for the things we do, but how wonderful when we are loved and even adored for just who we are. The only way a living soul could come into God's presence to love and worship the Father, and be a true glory to Him, would be for that soul to do so by his or her own desire to do so. Being created to worship and love God, with no other option, would be something artificial—lacking in earnestness. Thus, while angels worshiping Him is pleasing and stimulating to God, I doubt it to be satisfying for the long haul.

God Creates Choice

The only conclusion to that situation was for God to do something difficult and an antithesis (opposition) to His Nature—He must create choice.[1] Choice meant that there would have to be another to choose or accept, as an alternative to Himself. It would have to be one not like Him, but one who was His opposite. Lucifer was at that time a beautiful angel, and he was called "The Star of the Morning," because of his radiant beauty[2]. He was jealous of God and prideful[3], or at least, he had the tendency to be those things, and he wanted to be God.

It is even hard to say, but the only way to provide souls a choice over Himself and His Righteousness, was that God had to create evil.[4] I don't believe God created evil with any kind of vindictive or sinister attitude, because that is not who He is. Instead, evil became a necessary tenant of the opposite position to the Throne of God. We can see that "position theory" just by looking at our own experience in grade school. Each time we advanced to another grade or class, the roles of "class clown," "Miss Goody Two Shoes," or "trouble maker" would always be filled, and often by different people. Seldom would a position go vacant. So, what God had to do, instead of designating a king of evil, was create the Law of Opposition and let the vacancy fill itself.

The Law of Opposition
Every thing was put into place: the land of perfection and blessing (Garden of Eden, earth), the seed of man (Adam and Eve), and the resident liar and deceiver—the Prince of Darkness guised as the Serpent. As innocently as possible, God did what was necessary—He created evil by creating the Law of Opposition, casting Lucifer (by his own tendency) to be the trustee of perversion and foul things, then He waited first for Eve, then Adam, to activate the testing of the souls of man, by their disobedience.

God did not cause man to sin. He did not cause Lucifer to be prideful. He does not direct Satan to do the things that evil desires, but He did give Satan a great power, which is less power than He has[5], but a great power, none the less. When Satan brought Hitler to his strength, he did so on his own, and in his own timing, by building pride, arrogance, and a feeling of superiority to the man, and then corrupting him with power. Likewise, the coming Great Tribulation will be Satan's ultimate attempt to annihilate God's own. He will do so, by his design and on his time table, and that is why even Jesus did not and perhaps still knows not—when the time of it will begin.[6] It is not God who brings the Great Tribulation, but God will use it to bring great glory to Himself and His Kingdom.

God Has a Plan

Bible scholars estimate that Adam and Eve lived in the Garden of Eden as long as 120 years before their sin, which brought God's curse upon the land, upon the serpent, and upon the lineage of man. God knew it would happen. He allowed it to happen, because He wanted more than anything, to be surrounded by those who love Him and love the worship of Him. In the same manner, He knows we are going to sin. He knows that it is not in our power to overcome sin, so even before He set this earth in motion[7], He had a plan to take upon Himself, through His Son Jesus, all the sin and suffering of the world[8], so that those who would choose Him, could have the hope of escape from the great magnetic pull of corruption and depravity that leads to the opposite of Salvation—Damnation.

The chasm between us and God is great. We who are born on this earth live between the extremes provided by the Law of Opposition. The Kingdom of Light, Righteousness, Creation, and Salvation finds its home at the Throne of God, whereas the Kingdom of Darkness, Evil, Destruction, and Damnation resides squarely in the Pit of Hell. Between those two invisible thrones, we live. It is a difficult place to live at times, but we have God's Holy Spirit available to us for comfort and guidance, His Word for instruction, and His Covenant of Blood for our Salvation[9]. However, in competition with our Redemption is the destructive force of Perdition(Hell). [10] Using all the tools of his position, Satan tempts, lies, perverts, and deceives us to believe all manner of disgusting schemes. Our choice of whom resides with us (whether the Holy Spirit or Satan's demons) is found in our actions. God's Spirit dwells in His praise,[11] and the demons operate in our lives when temptation is tasted and dwelt upon.

The Big Picture, then, is a created world of Heaven and Earth brought into play at the same time as the Law of Opposition is set like a trap. The spiritual world is divided in the same way the waters on the face of the deep were divided, God in Heaven, and Satan in Hell—waiting for the testing of the soul of man to begin. The fall of man triggered the plan of God, and each of us afterward received a great gift—Choice. Inherently though, choice, wrapped in the package of original sin, brings pain and suffering along with joy and happiness. Though few recognize the beauty and value of this gift, some even throw it away by suicide; others squander it in pride and lustful living. It is a gift of incomparable excellence, that we have the opportunity to live as "Chosen" among the glories that God has in store for those who choose His Son, even suffer unto death, in order to love and worship the King, in Heaven, which is on the earth to come, at the end of time.[12]

THE SCOOP ON SATAN

The things I have talked about up till now are not so new, but may be presented in a fashion that is different from what you are used to hearing from the Sunday Pulpit. It will be the same for this chapter, as we talk about Satan and his christ. However, I am going to amplify the descriptions of him, because until now, he hasn't been given enough credit. When was the last time you heard a vivid description from the pulpit about the Liar and Thief? I am a subscriber to the axiom, "Hold your friends close, your enemies closer." As we study the Great Tribulation, and even talk to friends and relatives about it, you will find that except for a wild exception, most everyone will say that the time of Great Tribulation is God's Wrath against those who don't "make the Rapture." However, in what they say—they make two large errors: The Great Tribulation is not the Wrath of God, and, the "Secret Rapture" is a misunderstanding of Scripture.

God brings punishment, wrath and judgment. He allows His people to suffer for His Namesake, knowing that their reward later will be grand, but the Great Tribulation is Satan's last hoorah. Furthermore, each reference to a "Rapture" is misunderstood as they are teachings of the Resurrection

unto Harvest of wheat and tares, whereby the wheat is separated to reward, while the tares are bundled for the destruction by fire.

Satan is Opposite and Less Than God

The most accurate description of Satan is derived from the
Law of Opposition. Just as when North was established,
South was the immediate reply. South becomes the negative pole, because North is the positive. From Issac Newton's
postulate, "For every action, there is an equal and opposite
reaction," we may observe what sometimes is not so obvious. Now while the reaction is not truly equal (otherwise
we would have a perpetual motion machine), it is nearly
so. For example: A bounced ball will not return to its original dropped position, but will almost do so if air pressure
is very high. Likewise, Satan has very much power, as given
from God, but it cannot achieve the level of the Creator, just
as a bounced ball cannot go higher than the position where
it started.

Equal and Opposite

We continually see this phenomenon in the spiritual world.
Prior to every Christian holiday, such as Christmas and Eas-
ter, the "world" introduces a new book, movie, or seculariza-
tion of that holiday that is purposed to discredit Christ Himself, or to minimize those holidays which should be events
of worship. In another sense, when we saw an onset of evil,
such as "9/11," whereby those committed to evil gave their
lives in order to kill as many people as possible, then immediately (just as a bounced ball hitting the floor), we saw others rush in to save as many people as possible, at the cost of
their own lives. This phenomenon of "equal and opposite" is
always found in the spiritual world.

The Bible is chock-full of such illustrations, as even God is bound to the laws of His own Creation. We need go no further than the birth of a son, and a promise of Israel to Abram and Sarai, [1] but not until after the covenant God made to Hagar and her son Ishmael to be the father of many nations.

The Offset Press

Another way to see "equal and opposite" is to know a little about printing. We are in the printing ministry and know well how the press works. Using the principle of "oil and water do not mix," but reject each other, the plate that contains the image to be printed comes in contact with both ink rollers and a water-blanket roller.

The media that makes up the image attracts and holds oil. Ink is made from soybean oil so it sticks to the raised media. The rest of the aluminum or composition plate, attracts water, and that water keeps the oil from sticking to it. As the plate comes in contact with the rubber mat, the image transfers to it, or "offsets," then the rubber mat transfers the "mirrored image" to the paper. The thing we will see time and again, is that "offset effect," especially when comparing how Satan operates in a reverse, or mirrored image, of the way God performs His acts.

Satan Can Only Imitate God

Satan is the antithesis of God, on a negative and lesser scale. Who and what God is, Satan is opposite and less than. Where God is Love, Satan is apathy (not caring), and in some cases—hatred. God is Truth and Light; Satan is a liar and the Prince of Darkness.

For our study of the times to come, it is important to know that while God is the Creator, Satan cannot reach that level—he can only imitate and pervert the created thing. God is intelligent, while Satan is sly and crafty. He is not smart, but a real opportunist.

Hunters often think of their quarry, whether it be fish, turkey or deer, as smart, but they are not smart. They just have keen senses and a great fear that is triggered by something recognized by their senses as "out of character" or "out of place."

We will see it played out in Scriptures, that just as God had His prophets (operating in power from above to perform miracles) and the Messiah, who is Christ, Satan does no less. He will bring his own messiah (savior of the world), who will be the Antichrist. He will be surrounded by his prophets[2] (maybe called "masters of wisdom"),[3] and he will come, not to free and give life to as many as possible, but to kill and enslave as many as possible.[4]

Where days are numbered in the modern world, as in September 11, 2001 "A.D.," for example, most likely, the Antichrist will (in keeping up with the Joneses) record time after his own name (change the times)[5], as in "The Year of Our Master, 6 T.B. (*T*he *B*east), for example. The Bible records the Antichrist's name only as "The Beast," and it will be given to him by the citizens of the world. They will actually nickname him "The Beast" because he will astound them by his crafty and clever political moves, which yield him vast power where none can stand against him.[6] Hold-out leaders will simply have to abdicate their authority and lead, to him, because of overwhelming power and position the world citizens will give him.[7]

When the Time is Right for The Antichrist

At the right moment, and it has to be a time when the world is in a position of want and desperation, resulting from a world-wide catastrophe of some sort—financial, violent outbreak of war, or natural/man-made disaster—Satan will push his man to the front. It won't be a happen-chance event, but something prepared for, hundreds, even thousands of years in advance. Viewing the New-Age website *www.share-international.org* gives insight to such a plan, but whether Benjamin Creme' and his followers have a lock on the new "coming leader" named "The Maitreya," or whether they are simply another diversion (just one of the many antichrists to watch for), we must wait and watch.

The first coming of God's Messiah, Jesus, Who is the Christ, came to save the world from sin's destruction. He came so that "whosoever will" could destine themselves as heirs to the King of Creation and live—eternally. Satan, in his move to imitate and rob glory from God, will, sometime in the near future, put his christ in the seat of authority. He will do so because he is and always has been jealous of God. He wants to be God, so this move will, in his mind, place him in that position where he is worshiped by the world.

Satan's Antichrist will come to deceive and enslave as many as possible, using to the maximum, all the craft in his vault of lies. He will perform actual miracles, and in cases beyond his reach (events in the heavenlies, past his realm of power "of the earth and the air above the earth"), he will simply claim that those things were done at his hand.

With those things in mind, can you now begin to question what we have been taught, that God brings the Great Tribulation? He knows it will come because He is omniscient and omnipresent (all knowing and all present), and He will use it to bring scores of souls to surrender at the Cross, but this action to rule the world is a sinister and evil plan that can only have one source—The Pit of Hell.

AN END-TIME PUZZLE: PUTTING IT TOGETHER

Putting together an old, used, 1,000-piece puzzle is a lot like understanding God's purpose and prophecy of the End of Times, especially when some of the pieces are missing, and when the picture on the box is partial—at best. And to make the task of assembly even more difficult, it seems that several puzzle pieces of the same design, but by different manufacturers, have been thrown in together with this puzzle. Duplicate pieces may appear different, but still fit, even though their special features make it seem otherwise. Thus, as we examine pieces that differ somewhat, but still fit properly, it is acceptable to stack them on top of each other.

Using our analogy of a puzzle, these pieces are Scriptures that speak of the same thing, but may be shaded differently or carry more or less information. We must know that the "picture on the box" is already designed, so our carving on the pieces, or breaking off tabs so they will fit, or even overlooking a huge void where pieces don't match, will only cause us to arrive at a conclusion that is contrary to the Master's Plan.

Assembling the Puzzle

As we begin to assemble the pieces of the puzzle, we must have a plan. First, we must turn all the pieces face up and group them by colors, shades, border lines, and "special features," as we realize each piece has value. When we look at Scriptures, we can do the same thing—we can identify descriptions, events, and people, and use those same items to mark their place in time. By doing that, we can fill in the blanks left by one writer, yet supplied by another. We would use the same process for any event, such as a war. By studying the accounts of different observers, we would look for a common thread, so we can see the war as one event and not several different wars that seemed similar.

For example: there are over one hundred Scriptures in the Old Testament that foretold of the coming Messiah. Each one tells a different side of the nature and timing of His Coming or of His ministry. Put together, you have a composite view of this single, wonderful event. Still, until that time of His Com-

Photo by Ron Kuntz

ing, there was much speculation of who to expect, whether He was to be the King of Israel who would rule from a throne, or a meek Savior who would enter Jerusalem on the colt of a donkey.

Today, we can see how all those prophecies were like a piece of a puzzle, except the picture isn't complete yet, and won't be until the Millennium of His Reign. The prophecies of His Return, each of them incomplete, paint only a part of the picture. No one account is complete and must be compiled with the others, or we make the mistake of having Christ return multiple times in order to satisfy all the descriptions and "emotions" of His Second Coming. So, like His coming as a Babe—once, His return also—is once. When Jesus said that He was coming again, He didn't say He was coming again—and again.

God's Word Brings Peace

It is exciting when you realize a couple things concerning God's Word that will bring peace, from simply knowing what the days ahead will bring, according to His Word. The good news is that He wants us to know, but He doesn't want everyone to know! Well, maybe that's the first piece of the puzzle that we need to handle together.

The question many seekers ask is: "Why doesn't God just come out and say what is going to happen?" The answer is, "He does," but the person He wants to spend eternity with, is one who wants Him and wants to know Him since He is Truth. There are many hypocrites who want to live with eternal blessing, but are not really crazy about the Truth of God. Those people are, and will be, deceived, and will be eternally separated from God. That will be hard for us to accept at first because of the things we have been taught, such as, "God wants me happy," and "I believe in Jesus—that's enough," or "If I asked Jesus into my heart (or) was baptized, then nothing can cause me to lose my soul." The truth is that the road to Heaven is narrow and few are the travelers. Jesus said that, "many will say, Master, we healed the sick and cast out demons in your name," but He will say, "Depart from me, for I knew you not."[1]

"Depart from me," will be the answer to many who think they are Christians; but instead, they belong to the apostate church, meaning that they will fall away at the *"hour of thy temptation."*[2] They will break in the middle because they believed in Him at a "surface level," but repentance and turning from sin was not in them, and a true belief in Him, that causes transformation and repentance, simply wasn't there! The Scripture that says, "No one can take our salvation from us,"[3] has been interpreted to mean— "Nothing we can do will cause us to lose our salvation."

As we handle this puzzle piece a little more, we see as we read II Thessalonians 2:11-12, something that will be a shock if we haven't seen it before: *"And for this cause God shall send them strong delusion, that they should believe a lie: That they all might be damned who believed not the truth, but had pleasure in unrighteousness."* That's right, God has given the truth in His Word, but many don't want to be led by the Holy Spirit, and most people are afraid of the Holy Spirit. They have been told by big men what the picture on the box will look like and they want to believe it so badly, that they will just hurry and place the puzzle pieces anywhere—truly believing that they will fit later.

Watering Down the Gospel
To accomplish God's purpose of separating the foolish from the wise (so as to not cast pearls before swine), God "sealed" the words of prophecy,[4] until He, Himself, takes the seals

off as the Holy Spirit reveals to the "Truth-Seeker" His un-derstanding. We can question that or we can accept it, but whatever we decide to do from this point on is in direct rela-tionship to our "fear of God." It has probably been in the last one hundred to one hundred fifty years, that the Gospel has been watered down from a "Fire and Brimstone" salvation message to a "Love, Grace, and Prosperity" salvation mes-sage. We have lost the picture that He is a Great and Terrible God, full of Grace and Love, but jealous and wrathful, as well.

The fact that people are combative to the truth or noncha-lant about the Return of Christ is evidence that the love of truthfulness is not in them. They have jokes like, "I am not a pre, mid, or post-Tribber, I'm a pan-Tribber, which means whenever Jesus comes back—it'll all pan out."

A Care-less Attitude
So many people tell me that all that "prophecy stuff" in the Bible doesn't apply to them, because Jesus is going to rapture them out of here before the bad stuff happens. This cavalier attitude is similar to the one that the Jews had about the coming of the Messiah—"He will come someday—whenever He is ready."

Jesus spoke to that care-less attitude as He entered Jerusa-lem. Because the Jews did not know the time of their visita-tion, when they had Daniel's prophecy that told them the ex-act number of years,[5] He pronounced this sentence on them: "*...And shall lay thee even with the ground, and thy children within thee; and they shall not leave in thee one stone upon another; because thou knewest not the time of thy visitation*" (Luke 19:44). Thus, being care-less or flippant about the day and timing of His Return seems vulgar or sacrilegious, but certainly sinful—like using the Name of the Lord in vain.

So, our understanding of the puzzle of the End-Times must include a true knowledge of His Character. It is also worthless to know the mechanics of the last days, yet make no journey to the Cross of Christ where we might find His Love and Redemption through repentance and surrender.

True Repentance
We will continue with the puzzle, but first, a thought about True Repentance. Concerning repentance, there is man's repentance, and then there is God's Repentance. You can say also that there is man's "sorrow" and God's "Sorrow," as meaning the same. Coming to my mind is the defendant at hearing the jury foreman declare the verdict of "Guilty." The defendant breaks down and cries, or even faints at the verdict and sentencing. This is man's sorrow, because man is sorry he got caught and punished—he is truly "sorry."

Then there is the picture of the defendant who shows regret and sorrow, either by his composure or tears, as the details of his crime are revealed before the court. Sorrow overtakes him and he is grieved to the point that he changes his plea from innocent to guilty and begs for forgiveness. This is God's "Sorrow," or True Repentance.[6]

Salvation is dependent upon God's "Sorrow" for our sin, knowing that we have offended Him and that the punishment due us is dependent upon His Mercy, not our defense, because we surrendered defense when we confessed our guilt and sorrow over it. An unrepentant soul who feels no need for God's Sorrow, because he doesn't see that he has done all that much wrong, walks without the fear of God— and straight to the gates of Hell.

Chapter 8

SORTING THE PUZZLE PIECES

Now we probably should start sorting pieces, and since I am intrigued with those that are marked by "special features," I'll grab a few and we can see if any fit nicely with each other. The border pieces can be sorted as we come to them. I have a couple interesting verses here: I Cor. 15:51-52: *"Behold, I shew you a mystery; We shall not all sleep, but we shall all be changed, In a moment, in the twinkling of an eye, at the last trump: for the trumpet shall sound, and the dead shall be raised incorruptible, and we shall be changed."* That is the glorious moment everyone who loves the Lord awaits—it's our Hope of Glory.

The first verse unmistakably talks about the exchange that will take place (whether we are dead or alive) when we shall be "changed." Our flesh and blood body is exchanged for a glorious new, flesh and blood body, and the corruption of our mortality is exchanged for incorruption. It will happen quickly, in the twinkling of an eye, not a blink, but quicker—like a flash.

Maybe this piece gives us more information about the urgency of Jesus' exhortation, that He is coming "soon" or "quickly." Had He said, "Any day now," we might be wondering by now; but Jesus, speaking through Paul, seems to clearly say that when He starts His Return—it won't be long, but "quickly" as though an eye "twinkling."

"I Come Quickly"

Readers of the Bible have interpreted "coming soon" and "I come quickly" as a sort of urgency, so as to be prepared for "any moment," and that is the proper way to live the Christian life. But now, 2,000 years after those words were spoken, urgency doesn't seem to be the reasoning for their use. Instead, "soon" and "quickly" seem to be reserved for the time of the Great Tribulation, when the Antichrist will say that he is the one they were waiting for, and to wait for another is meaningless. Of that time, there will be a famine of His Word—there will be great tribulation and suffering.

To the Christians, "I come quickly," will be very meaningful, because they will need the assurance of the great day of His Coming. Jesus and the Apostles tell us to be ready now, because, once it starts, once the trumpet sounds, there will be no opportunity for a quick prayer or baptism. Like a click, snap, or twinkling—the beginning is the end.

So, I think we can accept the possibility that the words of urgency are now being held in "escrow" as chits or promissory notes to be "cashed in" when the time comes that we will desperately need the promise of His "Soon Coming."

The Last Trump

There is a large protruding segment from this I Corinthians puzzle piece, and I think its purpose is like a vending machine key that has a hollow shaft so it can't be easily duplicated or function in the wrong place, and that segment is "at the last trump": *"for the trumpet shall sound, and the dead shall be raised incorruptible."* It would be well to note that "the" is used, instead of "a" when pointing out the trumpet, for it isn't just "a" trumpet, but it is "the" trumpet. The reference to the "last" trump complexes the piece further, because it is not a random trumpet blast, but the last of a series.

Which series is it? There was a series of trumpet soundings when Joshua and the priests and choir members circled Jericho, once a day for seven days, but on the seventh day, seven blasts—and the last one was followed by a great shout by all the people. Then the walls fell straight down—into the earth. The only other series of trumpet blasts is in The Revelation of Jesus Christ, chapter 8, verse 6: *"And the seven angels which had the seven trumpets prepared themselves to sound."* These soundings that follow, seem to come closely to each other, perhaps a day or so apart, like those at Jericho. Each trump brings about an action from Heaven, and no less than when the seventh angel sounds, followed by a great shout: *"And the seventh angel sounded: and there were great voices in heaven, saying, The kingdoms of this world are become the kingdoms of our Lord, and of his Christ; and he shall reign for ever and ever."*[1] That action from Heaven is the culmination of the general Harvest of souls and gathering of tares for destruction. It is God's purpose for us—The Hope of Glory.

Here—Christ has come—and it is no secret. Revelation 11:18 tells of those who saw His Coming, but whose garments were soiled with unrepentant sin. *"And the nations were angry, and thy wrath is come, and the time of the dead, that they should be judged, and that thou shouldest give reward unto thy servants the prophets, and to the saints, and them that fear thy name, small and great; and shouldest destroy them which destroy the earth."* Clearly, this is the great event we have awaited, but additional clarity to an item of confusion is before us now: The nations were angry because His Wrath was upon them now, and they just realized it! The Wrath of God is not in the days that precede the coming of Christ, which are the Great Tribulation, but after.

A Scene in Heaven

The next verse, 19, sketches a view that might well be the "picture" on the cover of the puzzle box. *"And the temple of God was opened in heaven, and there was seen in his temple the ark of his testament: and there were lightnings, and voices, and thunderings, and an earthquake, and great hail."* In Revelation 11:15, when John saw these things that are yet to happen, they were quick and all of a sudden. It must have seemed to John that it happened all at once, but he had to record them as a chronological event, or otherwise he would have had to stack words on top of each other.

For example, verse 17 was the fulfillment of what the "first voice" showed him would happen in Revelation 4:10, *"The four and twenty elders fall down before him that sat on the throne, and worship him that liveth for ever and ever, and cast their crowns before the throne."* John saw it as prophecy of what was to come, then he saw it as prophecy completed.

I must take a pause here, because these words will resemble a "train wreck" in our mind, if we are not reading along in the Instruction Manual (our Bible) for this puzzle(see back of book). You see, when I picked up a piece of the puzzle that had "special features," some other pieces seemed to cling to it and they are putting themselves together.

Without jamming the pieces together, but allowing them to flow naturally as Truth builds on Truth, we can see an image forming. For example, Revelation 4 starts out calmly and has the purpose of preparing John, and us, as well, for seeing the events that are yet to occur, so "the Scene in Heaven" is like orientation day for college students. Here is the Throne of God, the jewels of Heaven, the beasts of worship, and the elders of God. It is more than we can comprehend at this time, but we need to orient ourselves to them now, because we'll see them again, and when we do, we will recognize them from our orientation.

Could This Be the Rapture?

These "special feature" pieces are still clinging together, and we have to treat them one by one or we will lose our place. Revelation 4:1 tells of a voice that is *"as it were a trumpet talking to me;"* and it said, *"Come up hither, and I will shew thee things which must be hereafter."* This voice must be the voice of Jesus, having qualities unlike any mortal or angel. When Jesus first addressed John in Revelation 1:15, it had *"the sound of many waters."* So as Jesus addressed John in his vision, and invited him to step deeper into understanding, by saying, *"Come up hither,"* He was physically taking John in the revelation, from Patmos, to Heaven. But the purpose of "coming up hither," was to show the things which are "coming later." It was orientation day, not graduation!

Many, perhaps most, prophecy puzzle teachers claim that this is the time of the Rapture of the saints, but how could it be? How could it be, without breaking off a protrusion of the I Corinthians 15:51 piece—the last trump? How could the Hope of Glory be recorded without a response of all Creation, even the damned? Only these words: *"Come up hither, and I will shew thee things which must be hereafter."* And that's it?

Is it possible that these "come up here" words, reference, or infer, the completion of God's Creation whereby the Hope of Glory has been realized? If that is it, isn't it an anticlimax, to say the very least? It is quite a scene for sure, as any view of Heaven would be, but the end of the age? Not hardly, whereas the Revelation 11:15 event, and following verses clearly record that day we call—His Return.

Chapter 9

DANIEL IDENTIFIES THREE GROUPS

A s I mentioned when we began this venture, in this large box of puzzle pieces are many pieces (verses) that are cut to fit, but may lack other information found in other pieces, or have information not found anywhere else. Because of their "special features," they will fit interchangeably with their counterparts, even though it is clear that they came from another writer.

One of the best examples of what I am describing is a verse found near the end of Daniel's prophecy of the end of days, Daniel 12:1,2: *"And at that time shall Michael stand up, the great prince which standeth for the children of thy people: and there shall be a time of trouble, such as never was since there was a nation even to that same time: and at that time thy people shall be delivered, every one that shall be found written in the book. And many of them that sleep in the dust of the earth shall awake, some to everlasting life, and some to shame and everlasting contempt."*

I have heard it said by many prophecy teachers that you

can't begin to understand the Book of Revelation until you understand the Book of Daniel, and this pair of verses is a perfect example of what they refer to. Daniel tells of a time, such as there has never been or will be (these words are used by several prophets to identify the Great Tribulation), and of the Angel of the Lord—Michael—who stands to deliver the Church (everyone who shall be found written in the book). Whether he is the one who sounds the final trump, or is the one who gives a shout (just as in the taking of Jericho), Michael is a player!

The Center of Our Puzzle
There is so much more! Note that there are at least three groups of people identified in Daniel 12:1, 2:

1. Many who sleep in the dust who arise to everlasting life.
2. The "some to shame and everlasting contempt" group.
3. An unmentioned group, but the counterpart, or offset to the "many" and conspicuous by their absence.

Do you see what I mean here? There is so much going on in these two verses, and each feature helps us see a large part of the picture already. This might be a good time to go fix a cup of coffee or glass of lemonade and "whew!" for a moment, because this pair of verses may go in the very center of our puzzle mat—and they may cover many other pieces that yield only partial information. In truth, most of the End-Time understanding is explained or implied in these two verses. They are the **mother-lode** of prophecy Scripture!

If I may summarize without interpreting for you, here is what I see happening: In the previous chapter, eleven, Daniel tells of the rule of the Antichrist, the Son of Perdition (Hell), and of his great holdings and power, then of trouble that threatens his rule, and of his end where none shall come to help him.[1] The trouble that threatens his rule must certainly be the realization of his suppressed knowledge of the Coming Christ.

The Dead are Raised

Then the beloved angel, Michael, stands for the children of God and delivers everyone whose name is written in the Lamb's Book of Life (Daniel refers to it only as "the book," because he has no knowledge yet of the Lamb of God who hasn't come yet as Messiah). But to **deliver** the children of God, they first must be resurrected, because most are dead (asleep). Now, those Redeemed who are asleep and those Damned who are asleep are raised to life.

Those who are dead in Christ meet Him in the clouds, followed immediately by those Redeemed who are still living through the Great Tribulation and have been awaiting His "soon" Return. They all are sealed for Everlasting Life and will spend the next, perhaps thirty days celebrating the Marriage Supper of the Lamb. At some time therein, Christ marks each one by **signing** His new Name on their foreheads.[2] The test for them is over: They are **signed, sealed and delivered.**

Meanwhile, the second group that was raised to shame and everlasting contempt does not ascend to Heaven, of course, but they stay put here on the earth, because the Father Himself, for thirty days will issue His Wrath as a promise to those prideful, unrepentant sinners who have rejected God's Son and His death on the Cross as payment for sin. Their shame will be at its highest point when they see Christ on a white horse, followed by ten thousands of Saints also on white horses, as they come in retribution, for the wrongs committed against the Father and the Son of God.

Finally, there appears to be the group that is obvious by their omission. While there are many who will arise to Everlasting Life, as well as those who inherit everlasting shame and contempt—there are some who are not a part of that "many." They might be many—more or less—but they are not part of groups one and two. They are neither the Redeemed nor the Damned. Speculation is the only option left for us here.

Fast Forward to The Millennium

In order to speculate who might not be raised, we need to find another piece of the puzzle that has the special feature of "unknown group." Since I have been working with this puzzle for a while, I am going to cheat and pick it out of the pile of border pieces, because it can function as both purposes. There is a period of time that the Bible gives little clear insight to (for the casual reader), except for Revelation 20, because there is nothing we can or need to do beforehand, that we don't need in preparation to live or die for Christ.

The Purpose of The Millennium

The thousand-year reign of Christ is called the Millennium. Its purpose escapes many Christians, but it is the "Victory Lap" of the race they have run and won.[3] Christ's reign as King in Israel is the seven-thousandth year after Creation, which means that it is the Sabbath, the Lord's Day, and it is for rest and worship. Following that thousand year time, the earth is destroyed and the new Heaven and Earth will come down (Revelation 21).

But before that time is over, Satan is loosed for "a little season." He shall go about to tempt the nations and "to deceive" the nations, and finally, Satan and those whose names were not written in the Lamb's Book of Life are cast into the lake of fire. His success **"to deceive"** is in question. He has already deceived multitudes, but of the Millennium souls, it is not known if he has success.

What Happens to the Rest of the Dead?

Now, for the unknown group in Revelation 20:5: *"But the rest of the dead lived not until the thousand years were finished. This is the first resurrection."* The "rest of the dead" cannot be those Redeemed because they were **signed, sealed and delivered** as we learned in Daniel 12:1, 2. Neither can they be the Damned at the first resurrection, because they will receive God's Wrath and join the Antichrist in Hell. It can only be those who were passed over at that time (group three). Now—for them—this is the first resurrection! Who can they be? Since they are neither the Damned nor the Redeemed for what they did with Christ, they must have been unable to do anything with Christ.

When I was a little boy, I thought I had one on my mother. She used every opportunity with her four boys to teach us something of God. Thinking far ahead and sure I had her boxed in, I asked, "Well, Mom, what about the Indians or other people who lived before Jesus and never even heard His Name?" It didn't take her long to assure me that, "Here's what I know, Tommy. I know that our Lord is a just and fair God, and He would not want anyone to suffer Hell until they first had a choice to accept or reject God's Son."

When Satan is Loosed

Now, we have a lot of traditions and things we tell to comfort one another at the loss of a loved one, especially if they were unable to know and decide who to worship. I must believe, though I haven't found the puzzle piece that cinches it, that group three, the unnamed group in Daniel 12:1, 2 and Revelation 20:5, are the ones whose "first resurrection" is a thousand years later than groups one and two. They can't live the victory lap with the Redeemed and they can't suffer the Wrath of God, because they aren't deserving of either. When Satan is loosed for that "little season," he possibly will deceive some of that "first resurrection," but certainly many of the others will see what life on earth is like when Christ is the King.

There is no clear indication in the Bible (that I can see), whether Satan is successful at his binge of deception, but I don't think so. Those who saw life under his rule as "god of this world," before, and now in the Millennium, will surely choose and surrender to God as they see that their second chance is one of pure, godly, Grace. They will also have the witness and encouragement of an earth full of evangelists, as martyrs will rule the provinces and good will prevail. Should they follow the Liar during that "little season" of temptation, after being given this extra measure of Grace, then little can be said in their defense. Today, in this immoral and perverted society, Satan has grand success and must feel superior; however, with Jesus as King, righteousness will have its proper place and when Satan comes to rob souls from the Messiah's Reign, he certainly will feel haggard and dejected.

Why is Satan Loosed?
Many of you, like my wife and I, have lost a baby or young child; perhaps you raised a child whom you knew was unable to make intelligent decisions—and when they are gone, we look for God's answer. Of those millions lost to abortion and unable to choose or reject Christ as their King, we tell ourselves things like, "Well, God must have needed a baby in Heaven," or something similar.

I think we can claim for certain that they will be treated as we are, and given a choice. This must be, because the purpose of Creation is to give "choice," so for eternity, God will be surrounded by those who have chosen and surrendered to God's sacrificial Lamb, by repentance. Otherwise, it would be as Heaven was before Creation, with angels worshiping because they were created to, or appointed by default to do so, not because they chose to.

Until the Lord brought this understanding to me, I couldn't understand the Millennium, nor "the rest of the dead," and why of all things, would Satan be loosed "for a little season?" If the damned had received the Wrath of God following the Great Tribulation, while the Redeemed drank the wine of the Marriage Supper, and the Bride of Christ, who did not worship the Beast or receive his image in their hand or forehead[4], shall rule and reign with Him for a thousand years, then who would there be to tempt? It would have to be, it could only be—those who have never had the opportunity to hear and trust upon the Name So Beautiful, Jesus.

A Lesson From Y2K
I am a keeper of little things that I might need one day. My pockets, drawers, truck ashtrays, and cup holders are full of nuts. bolts, clips, and other keepers that I might need sometime. Much the same way, I have been carrying in my mind, something I learned in the year 2000. It was the year of Y2K, which carried warnings of doom and such.

This information that I have been carrying was issued by the National Geographic Society, and it simply said that with their population studies, the year 2000 marked a sort of population equinox, which meant that at that time, the number of people alive was equal to the number of people who had ever lived. I didn't understand the prophecies of the Last Days then, so the fact that the number of people walking on the earth equaled the number who were asleep in the earth didn't have meaning to me.

I have been holding that information now for twelve years, and I need to use it. It is not so meaningful as evidence, but as light over an entire picture. It gives relevance to the vast number of people who could be members of the unknown in group three. On the other hand, we see a huge number of people who are alive today and those who have lived during the past two-thousand years, most of whom have heard the Gospel and gone to their graves with it being either their only Hope, or something they placed little value on.

A Promise and a Fulfillment

The Millennial Reign of Christ will come as a promise and as a fulfillment of prophecy. Jesus will be King of kings, and Lord of lords, and Satan, His enemy, will know it. The Damned will know it also and victory will last as a showcase of His Righteous Law, for one thousand years.

The Redeemed will have glorified bodies, which can mean several things to us. Since the earth will be reshaped, it seems that restoration of what the earth was before the curse that sin brought, is what we might expect. So, reshaping most likely will be "restoring." Then, our bodies most likely will be restored to the glory of our former created bodies—before sin. That looks good to me: Strength, thick hair, endurance, size, hearing and visual acuity—as God first intended, and health due to earth's original oxygen-rich environment; all the things we desire now, and instead of worrying about the next president or who will rule in congress, we will have a King On High, whom we will love and worship continuously.

There is much speculation about what we will do during that thousand years. Most likely, we will be working and enjoying the fruits of our labor. Swords and instruments of war will be beat into plowshares[5] so crops will be grown. Glorified seeds will replace genetically altered seeds and

produce healthy food. There will be no need to spray herbi-
cides and pesticides, because the curse of pests and disease
will be lifted.

Like you, I could speculate all day about the advantages of
living on the earth for a thousand years under the rule of
the King of kings; then after that, living on a new Earth and
Heaven forever, which is Heaven on Earth. But it serves little
purpose if we are fooled and deceived into believing something else. That is the purpose of this project—to prepare
everyone who doesn't want to miss the Good Life.

Chapter 10

THE FIRST AND SECOND RESURRECTION 🔧

Something that I do, which is related to keeping my pockets and drawers full of neat little clips and fasteners, is keeping my hands full. When working on a project, I might have two or three sockets, nuts, bolts, and a screwdriver in my hands while trying to fit two parts together. I just don't have enough hands. I have that feeling right now. Before I can go forward, I have to put some things down—so my mind will clear and so we can handle this next very important puzzle piece.

The First-Fruits of the Harvest 🔧

In Jesus' day, the harvest was completed in phases, a little like it is today. In those days, the "first fruits" were gathered[1] and taken to the temple as a tithe or guilt offering. This was done so God would get His, off the top. The phases of the harvest weren't mixed together. The second phase was the general harvest—that's what the farmer received for his labor. The third phase was what was left in the field for the poor to come and pick for themselves. It could be grain heads (like an ear of corn) that had been dropped and left, or it could have been short rows at the corner or end of an field. This phase is called "the gleanings," and that means everything useful that was left, omitted or slipped through the cracks, was gleaned and not left to perish. The gleanings phase most likely would take some time to be completed. Today, many farmers practice the third phase of the harvest by leaving rows of crop near the creek or tree line, so wildlife won't have such a struggle through the winter.

The Bible Speaks of Two Resurrections
There are two general resurrections in the Bible: The first is
that of **the Harvest**[(2)] and the second is **the Resurrection unto Judgment**.[(3)] The second resurrection is for the unredeemed and is to be avoided at all costs, because those resurrected unto Judgment will face the full brunt of rejection and punishment.

As I mentioned, the Resurrection of the Harvest will come in phases and over a great period of time, three thousand years, to be precise. Again, most doctrine comes close, but misses the mark by one thousand years, as the length of Harvest. We have always known that Christ represented the "First Fruits" of the Resurrection.[(4)] Unto God, Christ is returned to the Father as a "guilt" offering on our behalf. There can't be any dispute of this fact.

The second phase of the Harvest is at the Second Coming of Christ when the dead in Christ are raised to Eternal Life, as those Redeemed and yet living meet them in the air, and the end of the age is marked. There is a large dispute of this event, as those who teach of a pre-Tribulation Rapture, believe that this general Harvest is a mysterious and secretive event that precedes the Great Tribulation, and the remaining

"Gleanings" phase represents those who are saved and martyred during the Great Tribulation. A Rapture preceding the Great Tribulation is a great thought, but there is no definitive scriptural reference that isolates that doctrine from the references of His Second Coming and Resurrection.

But What About the Rest of the Dead?

That would complete the "Harvest" of the saints, in the thinking of those teaching pre-Tribulation Rapture, except—when they come to read Revelation 20:5, *"But the rest of the dead lived not until the thousand years were finished. **This is the first resurrection.**"*(bold added). Most of us, even seasoned Bible students, just read over the last five words of that verse because they don't make sense—placed there at the end of the thousand year reign of Christ. Jesus is revealing to John in this verse, that **THIS IS THE FIRST RESURRECTION** brought to completion. It is finished now!

Although it takes three thousand years to complete, this last piece of "rest of the dead" to be raised, represents the "Gleanings" phase of the Harvest, and now—it is completed. Those who are represented by this group, are certainly not the First Fruits, because that is Christ's position, and—they are not the Redeemed of the general Harvest at the coming of Christ, and neither are they the Damned, but are the "others" whom for some special reason did not have opportunity to know and accept Christ as their sacrifice and Savior.

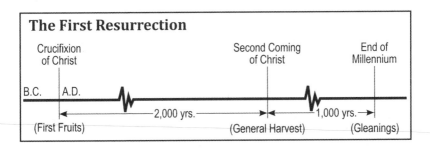

The Second Resurrection

The First Resurrection is complete then, as we have just seen, at the end of the thousand-year reign of Christ on earth. Then Satan is loosed for a little season of time,[(5)] in order that he might provide choice to those now living, but not "sealed" by Christ, they include those born during the Millennium as well as the third group. Some, perhaps, will be deceived and follow the Serpent to destruction.

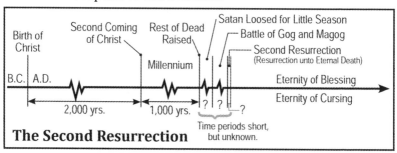

The final battle will commence, as Satan declares war against God Himself,[(6)] but before the first shot is fired, God sends fire down from Heaven and the enemy is destroyed. Satan loses big time. Then all activities of separating the sheep from the goats and the purpose of Creation is finished. Those now dead, are dead because they followed the wrong master. They belong to Satan and the Pit. They are then resurrected to Judgment, and after their deeds are read from the Book, and before all the world, they are condemned to everlasting fire and torment. That is the second death—which is eternal death.[(7)]

The Judgment after the Second Resurrection does not determine guilt or innocence—that is done by action of each soul before death: Judgment is purely the "sentencing phase" of the trial where the books of the deeds of men are opened and read. They will be condemned and sentenced by what they did with Christ and for the sin that they chose to keep to themselves.

TIMING IS EVERYTHING

E veryone has heard the old adage for where to place a business: Location, Location, Location. In other words, no matter what you do or how well you do it, if you are in an inconvenient or inappropriate location—your business will suffer. Whether you are in business or simply want to prosper in what you do, I offer that greater than location, "Timing is everything."

Tom at his salvage yard, preparing a container load of supplies — headed for Haiti.

Since Christ ascended into the clouds, leaving the promise of His soon return, the discussion of timing has been on the "eye-level" shelf, and that is where it belongs. When I operated an auto recycling yard several years ago, I had an order for a low mileage 2.2 Chrysler engine. I had just the thing, but it was in a badly damaged car. Bobby, one of my dismantlers, "unwrapped" the engine by peeling away all the crushed metal from around it, but noticed that the timing belt had been cut, so he replaced it with a new one. He tried to test-fire the engine for many hours, but as it tried to run, it could only get warm, make running sounds, and nearly run. We tried everything, even rechecking the timing marks often.

"Hmmm"

After several hours I restudied the timing marks with a good light. Both large marks were matched; however, I noticed a much smaller mark on the crankshaft that was purposefully set, but barely noticeable. Bobby strongly resisted my instruction to him to reset the timing to the "acute" (smaller) mark, but after he did, he hit the starter and we heard "Hmmmm." Bobby smiled so hard, it turned to laughter. The engine was pulled and sent to the customer, never to be heard from again.

Now, that is a longer story than I wanted to spend time on here, but its value has no equal. The engine had all the components of its purpose: fuel, air, compression, and was the result of decades of engineering, but lacked timing to the degree of one tooth. If we were not tenacious (unrelenting) in our search for the needed timing, the sale would have been lost, and the engine scrapped! Need I say more about the value of our tenacity concerning the timing of the Lord's Return?

We are not arguing or leveling a finger at each other, but we are trying to find two marks that match. In doing so, I have tried to keep everyone in our ministry on the same wagon as we bump down the road of discussion. Some keep falling off the wagon and I couldn't understand why, since the clarity of evidence seems overwhelming to me. Reading the letters from many of them, I realized a clear pattern of understanding that is like the two large timing marks. To our understanding, they clearly match, but the engine won't run on its own, without teachers to tell us what things mean.

Tribulation, Wrath, and Judgment
That one large mark that keeps us out of time, is the definition of the Great Tribulation. While false teachers call it God's Wrath, even God's Tribulation, THEY TEACH A MARK ILL PLACED, and all it yields is "heat and noise." The Bible does not teach that—anywhere. Yes, God does send curses and judgments to the ungodly and to the Antichrist, but that is in response to what they do to Israel, the Jewish people, and "the remnant of her seed," the saved Gentiles. He does that just as He sent curses upon Pharaoh and his Egypt for the cruelty and oppression heaped on Israel whom he held in bondage.

Do you think Jesus brings tribulation on people? No, but He will release a second installment of God's Wrath one day, and the Father will bring Judgment on another day, but let us not confuse those terms. Tribulation, Wrath, and Judgment are three distinct items, coming separately, and not at random times, but like a clock and a calendar, and not one tick out of sync.

1. The **Great Tribulation** comes not at God's Hand, but like the Great Holocaust: Satan sends his apostle to do his work

of destruction, as his attempt to cancel God's Work and His People.

2. God's **Wrath** is witnessed when He has had enough. It builds like a river dammed up by His LONGSUFFERING. When that dam breaks, things get ugly—fast. It came in Noah's day when sin and disobedience was the mainstay for the people. It will happen once again after Jesus returns, and the Redeemed (dead and living) are resurrected to Eternal Life, while the damned are resurrected also, to shame and everlasting contempt, but also to receive the Wrath of God (Daniel 12:2).

3. God's **Judgment** comes after the Millennial Reign of Christ on earth, after the Second Resurrection.

Does Jesus Return Once or Twice?

The discussion about whether Jesus returns once or twice before the Millennium is one of timing. We must be able to read the timing marks thoroughly or suffer the poverty of ignorance (not knowing). Recently while reading a pre-Tribulation Rapture book, *"The Master Plan,"* by David Reagan,[1] I saw one of those large, misleading timing marks. He used the verses found in Jude 14, 15: *"...Behold, the Lord cometh with ten thousands of his saints, to execute judgment upon all..."* to promote the doctrine of a pre-Tribulation Rapture, with Jesus at His Second Coming, bringing His saints with Him to execute Judgment.

Reagan then infers that the saints are retrieved from an earlier rapture. To his thinking, that cinches the Doctrine of pre-Tribulation Rapture. For me, it brings back the same feeling I had when Bobby and I stared at that engine and felt it getting warm, but we were unable to ship it because it wouldn't run. Looking with a good light at those two verses, we see the little mark—it is judgment with a small "j." Judgment (with a capital J) doesn't come until the Millennium is complete, but when the Lord comes with ten thousands of His Saints, it will be a judgment of wrath that the Son of God delivers, judgment that culminates with the Battle of Armageddon.

While Dr. Reagan uses those verses to teach an earlier rapture, he unconsciously, but correctly places God's Wrath beginning at the Return of Christ (Revelation 11:15). He does so by using "judgment and wrath" interchangeably, but at the expense of accuracy. When you identify Tribulation, Wrath, and Judgment separately, and give them their proper timing, the result is a joy in Truthfulness and the sound you have sought for years: "Hmmmm."

An Advance-Level Puzzle
In defense of dedicated Bible scholars and lovers of God's Word, such as the one I just mentioned, we must realize the complexity of prophecy. I used the analogy of a "one-thousand piece puzzle" for our understanding, then added the complication of additional puzzle pieces from other manufacturers thrown in, which accounts for stacks of pieces fitting on the same mat, but looking somewhat different. But, there is an additional complication that I can't find an analogy for—it comes about simply because at several points of John's vision, there is simply a lot of action taking place. You can't cram everything in the same chapter—there's just too much. So when he brings it up later, we tend to think it happened later. Such is the case with Revelation 19:11-21.

11. "And I saw heaven opened, and behold a white horse; and he that sat upon him was called Faithful and True, and in righteousness he doth judge and make war.
12. His eyes were as a flame of fire, and on his head were many crowns; and he had a name written, that no man knew, but he himself.

13. And he was clothed with a vesture dipped in blood: and his name is called The Word of God.

14. And the armies which were in heaven followed him upon white horses, clothed in fine linen, white and clean.

15. And out of his mouth goeth a sharp sword, that with it he should smite the nations: and he shall rule them with a rod of iron: and he treadeth the winepress of the fierceness and wrath of Almighty God.

16. And he hath on his vesture and on his thigh a name written, KING OF KINGS, AND LORD OF LORDS.

17. And I saw an angel standing in the sun; and he cried with a loud voice, saying to all the fowls that fly in the midst of heaven, Come and gather yourselves together unto the supper of the great God;

18. That ye may eat the flesh of kings, and the flesh of captains, and the flesh of mighty men, and the flesh of horses, and of them that sit on them, and the flesh of all men, both free and bond, both small and great.

19. And I saw the beast, and the kings of the earth, and their armies, gathered together to make war against him that sat on the horse, and against his army.

20. And the beast was taken, and with him the false prophet that wrought miracles before him, with which he deceived them that had received the mark of the beast, and them that worshipped his image. These both were cast alive into a lake of fire burning with brimstone.

21. And the remnant were slain with the sword of him that sat upon the horse, which sword proceeded out of his mouth: and all the fowls were filled with their flesh."

After the description of God the Father's Wrath and fallen Babylon, John goes back to share what happened during the next 45 days of God's Wrath, which was brought by The Son and His Bride after the great celebration Marriage Supper and Marriage. The gathering of saints for the Son's portion of wrathful judgment is the second part of the Wrath of God which ended at Armageddon.

For example: The Scriptures we previously looked at (Jude 14, 15) are cut in a similar fashion as those in Revelation 19:11-21, but don't give as much detail. I almost could throw up my hands and say, "I just don't get some of it," but I know that there are no contradictions in God's Word. That knowledge is a great help right now, as I handle the pieces of this puzzle and anticipate greatly the time when I can be with the Lord.

Spans of Time
In the Book of Revelation, the apostle John is recalling and writing from a vision from the Lord. He can't go back and quote Scripture to build his case, he just writes it as he sees it. Also, as in the case of Daniel and other prophets, there are "spans of time" in a description, that aren't measured out for us. So, we rearrange pieces as they become more complex and intricate.

In handling the puzzle piece of Revelation 19:11-21, we see the robe of Jesus, dipped in blood, and we see His armies following Him, all on white horses. This can't be the Second Coming of Christ, because it follows the Marriage Supper of the Lamb (verses 7-10), nor is it the Judgment which comes later, after the Millennial Reign (Revelation 20:11-15).

Early on, I echoed what many have said before me, that "you can't understand the Book of Revelation until you have a good grasp on the Book of Daniel." Why? Because Daniel says things about the events at hand, that John doesn't mention. I have tried to get a grip on the apparent vague reference by Daniel of the time past the alloted 1260 days of Great Tribulation, the 1290 days and then again, the 1335 days (Daniel 12:11,12).

There are 1260 days alloted for the Great Tribulation. Then there is an an additional thirty days, and then another forty-five day period of time. To complicate things further, Daniel declares that "blessed" are the ones who keep waiting and attaining[2] to the end. I must understand that it is not those left to endure the Wrath of God following the Great Tribulation, who "wait and attain to the end," but those who wait with the Groom and attain "sealed status" as a result of the Marriage Supper.

I explained earlier in this writing, that I thought of that "extension" of Wrath as a "letting it all out" kind of beating that He gives those who, with their lives, crucified His Son, in their words, deeds, and rejection of Him. I see it that way, but issued like a tag-team event. It's a family matter, and I will explain it here:

The Key for Assembling the Final Pieces
It is all about relationships. Once, a group of pseudo-religious leaders made a charge against my son's father (me). He saw red, but tempered it with "confrontation through reason." The stand he made caused the accusers to see the light, because he clearly defended the father on the grounds of what he knew about his character, not on what they charged him with.

In the same way, no one is going to hurt my son, daughter, or wife—or even slander them—without at some time wearing me for a while. It may not come immediately, but it will come. One other time, as a young boy, I came to my mother complaining about a stranger who had visited our neighborhood and had done some nasty things to me. Her movements were a blur as she found a baseball bat and scoured the neighborhood for anyone who didn't belong there. It was probably animal instinct that told the man that there was danger in the air, because my mother returned with a clean bat.

Could it be, that following the reign of terror by Satan, his christ, and their crowd against the:
Chosen Race;
the Redeemed of Christ;
the Appointed Witnesses;
the Holy Jerusalem;
the unholy assault on the earth and those who dwell on the earth;
and the Abomination of Desolation;
that the Father Who sits on the Throne wants the first crack at all the ones of evil? (Isaiah 63:1-6).[3]

Knowing what you know about family, can you see God's Son then coming to finish off what the Father started, and bringing with Him those who were faithful and who also received persecution and tribulation at the hands of evil? Together, with a rod of iron, the "stranger in the neighborhood" is dealt with and the score is settled.

Seeing that happen, after the bonding that occurs at the thirty days of the Wedding Feast, can you now see what Jesus meant when He went upon a mountain to speak to the multitude, these words, which until now just seemed like "flowery talk," but instead, are the most revealing prophecies of the time of: Resurrection, Marriage, Wrath, and the blessing of the Millennium and the New Heaven on Earth?

"Blessed are the poor in spirit: for theirs is the kingdom of heaven.
Blessed are they that mourn for they shall be comforted.

Blessed are the meek: for they shall inherit the earth.
Blessed are they which do hunger and thirst after righteous-
ness: for they shall be filled.
Blessed are the merciful: for they shall obtain mercy.
Blessed are the pure in heart: for they shall see God.
Blessed are the peacemakers: for they shall be called the chil-
dren of God.
Blessed are they which are persecuted for righteousness' sake:
for theirs is the kingdom of heaven.
Blessed are ye, when men shall revile you, and persecute you,
and shall say all manner of evil against you falsely, for my sake.
Rejoice, and be exceeding glad: for great is your reward in
heaven: for so persecuted they the prophets which were before
you."

Jesus said, *"I am the Resurrection and the life..."*[4] and the power that is in His statement grants what we have always known as the "Beatitudes," now as prophetic articles of Redemption. We win and we who are overcomers of sin, will ride with Him for forty-five days. We will have waited and attained Redemption to the end, and now we also mete punishment to those who have killed, maimed and assaulted that which is God's, as He stood for us, we then will stand for Him!

THE TIME LINE

We all would like to see on paper what the puzzle of the End Time events will look like, so now, using text and graphics, we will offer a visual map of possible scenarios for the rise and fall of the Antichrist and of the very specific times for events to occur. The prophetic events are multiple and interrelated, like puzzle pieces, but before we list them, I want to tell you about rabbit hunting.

Modus Operandi

A seasoned rabbit hunter will tell you that you should use a short and slow dog like the Beagle to sniff out a rabbit and put him to flight. The Beagle is slow, so the rabbit takes his time and runs in a large circle, coming back to the place where he began, and the hunter simply notes where the rabbit jumped up. Then, with weapon poised, takes his shot. Knowing the nature of the rabbit makes the hunt predictable.

Each of us behaves predictably; our thought patterns, experiences, and nature cause us to "take the same trail," time after time. That's why law enforcement agencies employ "profilers" to bring difficult cases to quick conclusions. You, I, God—even Satan—are beings of habit. It's like forgetting what we were doing so we go back and retrace our steps, hoping it will come back to us, because we have a way of doing things, always the same way.

God Knows Satan's Every Move

God, the original profiler, can know Satan's every move, because He knows who he is. He knows and can prophesy through His prophets, the very thing Satan will do. Like a rabbit hunter, He knows that Satan (formerly Lucifer) wants to be God and have God's things for himself, and to destroy that which he can't have. Knowing that, God can predict every move and action of Satan or his soldiers, including the Antichrist.

When Jesus left Jerusalem "desolate," it would be just a matter of time (2,000 years) before Satan's christ will come to occupy it. When he does, he brings the thing that he is: Abomination. When Daniel spoke of the "abomination of desolation," he was using God's Words, because these things were well ahead of his time. Jesus first used the term Himself shortly after He spoke of the desolation He left (was in the process of leaving) as He would go to the Cross. [1]

When to Expect Christ's Return

Now, Jesus said that only the Father knows the hour that the Son Of God will return.[2] He knows, because He is omnipotent (all knowing). Now when Jesus said that even He didn't know, we must assume that since He too, is God, then He would at sometime know. Maybe it would come after He was resurrected or after the Antichrist is revealed, but well beforehand, He would know.

It would follow, that we, also, can and will know, by the proximity of the yapping Beagles, when to expect Christ's Second Coming. Maybe not by the very hour or very day, but close to that. I am certainly not recommending that we "fix times," but once the Antichrist does certain things, then preset calendars kick into place. They must follow, by Satan's imitation of God's way and timing. God's number of completion is SEVEN, so the timing of the rule of Satan's christ is: Seven years.

The First Calendar—Jacob's Trouble

The most infamous calendar in prophecy is "The Time of Jacob's Trouble." It is known also as Daniel's 70th week of years.[3] The first sixty-nine years of Daniel's seventy weeks of years foretold of the coming of the Messiah—the birth of Christ—four hundred-eighty-three years (or sixty-nine weeks of years) after Daniel's prophecy. The unused week is reserved for Christ's Second Coming and is activated by the Antichrist.

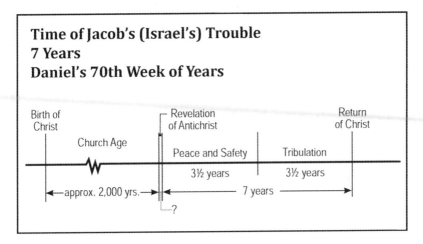

Time of Jacob's (Israel's) Trouble
7 Years
Daniel's 70th Week of Years

Birth of Christ — Church Age — approx. 2,000 yrs. — Revelation of Antichrist — Peace and Safety — 3½ years — ? — Tribulation — 3½ years — 7 years — Return of Christ

He activates the calendar when he makes a Covenant of Peace with Israel—for seven years. You might see that, as a rabbit jumping up from a clump of grass, because that starts the clock ticking. Nothing can change the outcome—seven years from that moment—The Hope of Glory, the kingdoms of Earth are become Kingdoms of God, Jesus has come. This seven year period is the last seven years of the Age of Grace, and it is the last seven years of the Church (the body of Christ on earth), but that is not the Great Tribulation, as has been taught for two-hundred years.

The Second Calendar—The Time of The Great Tribulation
There is a time within that seven year calendar—half in size, measuring three and one-half years. It marks separately the last half of the Time of Jacob's Trouble, because, as Jacob, "Israel,"[4] has seen relative peace resulting from the Covenant with the Antichrist, for the first half of this covenant time. All that changes when he sets his diabolical plan into action. He does that by traveling to Israel, and with the backing of the Gentile armies—He stands on the Holy Place and declares himself to be God.[5] He curses and mocks the God of Heaven, then he forbids the daily sacrifice by the Jews. He then orders the annihilation of all Jews. This action initiates the Great Tribulation

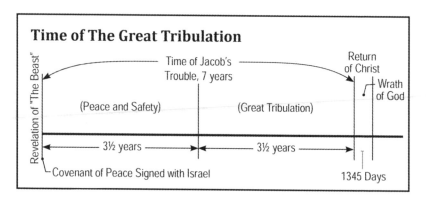

Time of The Great Tribulation

Revelation of "The Beast"

Time of Jacob's Trouble, 7 years

Return of Christ

Wrath of God

(Peace and Safety)   (Great Tribulation)

◄──── 3½ years ────►◄──── 3½ years ────►

Covenant of Peace Signed with Israel   1345 Days

The Abomination of Desolation
The name for this action of coming to Israel is given first by Daniel as: THE ABOMINATION OF DESOLATION.[6] It is thereafter referred to in prophecy by Jesus and those following Him as the moment that activates our second calendar, well known as the GREAT TRIBULATION.[7] You could compare that time as 180 degrees of the 360 degree rabbit circle. It doesn't begin until the seven year journey is half finished.

Up until now, we have been trying to put these pieces together as pieces of a puzzle, all fitting nicely in the imprint of the mat which comprises the puzzle, but from here on out, pieces will have to stack on top of each other: The Great Tribulation fitting on top of The Time of Jacob's Trouble, covering the last half of it, and kind of glued together with the Abomination of Desolation.

What's in a Name?
The Abomination of Desolation is not something you find on a shelf at a Walgreens. It is a name of special meaning and causes the newcomer to start looking out the window, so as to say, "I am not ready for all this, this is too weird." I am not so new, having been in this for decades—and that is what I said, until I turned back a chapter.

In a well-worn page of my Bible, Matthew 24:15, we see Jesus' first use of the "A" word: *"When ye therefore shall see the abomination of desolation, spoken of by Daniel the prophet, stand in the holy place..."* In that usage, abomination is used as a verb, noun, and pronoun. Let me explain: the Antichrist is an abomination, he is The Abomination, and what he is doing, is an abomination.

The Second Part of It
Desolation is a word we can handle easily by itself. For example: *"The doors and windows were gone, as the old town was left to desolation, many years ago after the shoe factory moved to China."* Desolation has the same lonesome sound as forsaken, neglected, and abandoned. Israel, and Jerusalem in particular have thus been forsaken by the pronouncement Jesus made just before the "Olivette Discourse" (as is called the time when Jesus answered the disciples' questions about the end and the signs of His Second Coming).

This puzzle piece is found in Matthew 23:38,39: *"Behold, your house is left unto you desolate. For I say unto you, Ye shall not see me henceforth, till ye shall say, Blessed is he that cometh in the name of the Lord."* Simply, Jesus was saying that He was turning the House of Israel over to them—desolate. He was leaving a void, as He—The Messiah—was leaving, and they would not see Him again until He came back (not under any other name either, but in the Name of the Lord).

So now we have an understanding of Abomination of Desolation: "The void left by Jesus at His Crucifixion, is to be filled by Abomination. The Antichrist is, and does the Abomination of Desolation, as no greater foul could be committed, than to stand on the Holy Place[8] and curse the God of Heaven, and claim to be God himself."

The Time of General Peace
The first half of the Time of Jacob's Trouble will resemble days like today for Israel, while the Righteous will no doubt anguish, to some degree, maybe even begin to suffer and become estranged from the world system under definite evil leadership. The other people will exclaim, "Peace and Safety,"[9] as they worship and languish under the Antichrist. At the end of the first part of Jacob's Trouble, when the Antichrist declares himself to be God, the Jews flee to the hills, caves and forests, with no more than the clothes on their back.[10]

Satan is foiled again, in his attempt to rid the world of Jews, so he turns his anger and venom against those reborn of Christ's Blood,[11] the Christians, and seeks to rid the world of them. There will be a sort of brand issued to the world citizens at that time, or maybe some before that time, which will separate those who worship the Antichrist, named by the people as the "Beast." This will be confirmation again of Daniel's prophecy.[12]

The Mark of The Beast
There have been many books written, most which are now outdated, that focus only on the Mark of the Beast. We won't spend that kind of focus here, because there is no need for speculation, but only God's Word and warning. The Mark of the Beast will be applied to the right hand, or in the case that a right hand is not available (or maybe for some other purpose of identification), it will be applied on the forehead.

Resistors are Shunned
The Mark of the Beast will enable the World Citizen to participate in commerce, health care benefits, education, and all the other benefits of today's society. Without the Mark, resistors will be shunned and violated as "animals." They will be the enemy of the world and treated as such. They will be on the run, hiding in fear, scavenging food and clothing, except where some have "put away" provisions for that day.

God will cause some who take the Mark, to be sympathizers, to aid and abet those on the run, like the underground highways and safe houses as were found during the Great Holocaust and during the dark days of slavery; while others will turn them in to authorities. The elimination of resistors will continually be ratcheted up, as those who will take the Mark of the Beast and worship the Antichrist, will increase in parallel with increased suffering. Those who cave in are the last of the Apostate Church (falling away).

chapter 13

THE TIME OF THE
GREAT TRIBULATION

The last three and one-half years of this age, "Jacob's Trouble," are defined by Daniel as, *"a time of trouble, such as never was since there was a nation even to the same time"*[1] Christians dread this time, because they have read the Book; pagans also know something is up, but there's comfort in a crowd, so they herd together and try to think everything is proper, just as German citizens did during Hitler's rule. The most widely taught theory, that of a pre-Tribulation Rapture, says that true Christians will be taken from this world to escape the Great Tribulation before the revelation of the Antichrist, and at Jesus' Second Coming they come back with Him "in mass" to retrieve those of the Great Tribulation who did not take the Mark of the Beast, and who did surrender to the Lordship of Jesus Christ.

I was taught this doctrine as I grew up in the Assembly of God denomination, and that continued as I was later a member of a Baptist church. I have preached it, taught it, and firmly believed it for fifty-plus years. My conversion is a long story that covered a short time, and the only thing of interest here is that, without any recognizable influence from anyone's teaching, overnight I was changed in my doctrine. I went to bed as a pre-Tribulation believer and woke up a Resurrection at His Second Coming, believer.

It was a near-violent bump in my road of life, and at the time of this writing—it has only been two and one-half years. Since then, I have had many of the people in our ministry come to me with Scriptures, books, tape sets, inferences, and "pictures" of the Rapture found in so many theorists of today, but in fairly examining all of it, there is not one thing that made me second guess or have a *déjà vu* moment that I was misled. That's because I have faith in the Lord that He opened my eyes, Himself.

Every Scripture I read now, that I read before, refers to the Second Coming of Christ at: the last day, the last trump, and the end of the age. I have utter and absolute confidence in the Second Coming of Christ, and complete dismissal of a rapture before the Great Tribulation.

The Witness of His Word is Truth

Changing overnight from a pre-Tribulation belief to post-Tribulation can only be accomplished by an action of the Holy Spirit. For some, like myself, it was nearly a violent conversion; for others, it is like shifting your weight from one foot to another. In whichever case, the good to be had is finally holding to your breast—the Truth of God. Then, the witness of His Word can be preached and taught, knowing that when that time comes, there is no need for adjustment in your witness and testimony.[2] And when the Mark of the Beast is introduced, we can know that it is the MARK OF HELL, with no amnesty for error—it is acceptance of Damnation and rejection of Christ.[3] Need I tell you to reject it at all costs?

Learning from the French Revolution

In 1793, France experienced a "snapshot" of what we might understand the Great Tribulation to resemble. It might even be considered to be a trial run by Satan, as he hones his plan for world domination.

Then Director of "Public Safety," Robespierre, sought to purify the population by suppressing resistance to the French Revolution. Marie Antoinette was the first to receive the "National Razor," as the Guillotine came to be called, and after her, in excess of 36,000 people lost their heads, with the last person being Robespierre himself succumbing to execution on 9 Therimidor Year II of the Revolution.

There is so much interesting material in this dark page of French history, and one doesn't have to read far to see that Satan has an M.O. and can be read like a book. Highlights of this era of French history are seen to be a prophecy of what the Great Tribulation will resemble.

1. One man coming in on the throes of claiming "Peace and Justice."[4]
2. Given the nickname of "The Incorruptible."
3. Execution of "uncooperative" by decapitation.[5]
4. Great numbers of lives lost.[6]
5. Citizens turned in suspected anti-revolution sympathizers.[7]
6. Complete dictatorial power. [8]
7. Political purges. [9]
8. Arrogance and pride by an absolute leader.[10]
9. The leader becomes intoxicated with the blood spilled by resistors.[11]
10. Movement ends at his death. [12]
11. Clergy required to take oath of loyalty to the nation. (Mark of the Beast)[13]
12. Times (calendar) changed to mark leader's rule. [14]

13. Rule ended with his death.

The Great Holocaust
Yet, there is another event in more recent history, that resembles the Great Tribulation. The Great Holocaust saw the execution of more than six million Jews.
1. Jews were labeled as "sub-human" and sent by rail to concentration camps throughout Europe.[15]2. They were treated in the most inhumane fashion, used for medical experimentation, tortured, used for target practice, and sexually abused.
3. The leader was prideful and superior to all, in his own eyes.[16]
4. Hitler sought to become the world leader.[17]
5. Given nickname "der-fuher," meaning "The Leader."
6. Hitler's enemy was God's Chosen.[18]
7. Hitler didn't instigate the Nazi movement, but followed the lead of Rosenburg and Goering.
8. Not only did he hate Jews, but Christians, as well, and anything pertaining to God. He forbid the wishing of "Merry Christmas" and recommended "Happy Winter Solstice" and "Winter Greetings," instead.
9. Clergy used to pacify the people.
10. Empire ended with his death, as righteousness overcame evil.[19]

The Antichrist
1. At some point early in the revelation of the Antichrist, he will *"wear out the saints of the most High,"* as he will speak great words against the most High.[20]
2. Comes as Man of peace, sharing, and justice, in imitation of Christ.[21]
3. Will walk in arrogance and pride.[22]
4. Will usurp power quickly and many will be amazed at his political maneuvers to overcome rivals.

5. The people will call him the "Beast" as everything he does swamps the imagination of observers.

6. According to the prophet Daniel, the Antichrist will attempt to change the "times" (most likely meaning calendars) just as Robespierre did, thus again imitating the Christ, as our years number forward and backward from His life. Also, Daniel said that he will change the "laws,"[23] and to this writer, it is not clear what that means. Certainly it doesn't refer to local municipal laws, but something much larger—like laws of science and of the Universe.

7. The enemy of the Antichrist will again be God's Chosen: both the Jew and the Elect, those not neglecting God's Law and His Word. At the beginning of the three and one-half year Great Tribulation, this assault will be in full swing.

8. The Antichrist will be "drunk" on the blood of the martyrs.

9. The rule of the Antichrist will be world-wide, there will be no place to hide, but it won't last forever.[24]

10. The Antichrist realizes that his rule is coming to an end as "the Righteous Hand" is coming after him, and the Great Tribulation ends when he is cast down to the Pit, at the Coming of Christ.[25]

The Beast

There will be difficult times ahead for anyone refusing to worship the Beast, a nickname given to the leader because his power will exceed any human in the history of the world. The term: "Beast" illustrates something awesome and beyond comprehension.

When the current U.S. President visited the United Kingdom in May, 2011, he took two Air Force jets and his personal Cadillac limousine, specially built by GM to be bomb proof, bullet proof, carrying its own oxygen supply and, among other things, specially reinforced tires. The British press immediately nicknamed the vehicle THE BEAST, because it was beyond anything they had ever seen.

An old expression states that large men talk about ideas and theories, while small men talk about other men. And so it will be with the world when the Antichrist either performs something "magical"[26] or out-maneuvers other political leaders, small people will admire and talk about him, and his power will greatly increase as people, like sheep, follow him to slaughter.

There will be a frenzy about him just as there always is about someone who holds "fascination," such as a Hollywood star or someone with greatness. And, as sayings continue: "Power corrupts, absolute power, absolutely corrupts." And this man who has the power of the people thrust upon him, making invisible the borders of today's nations, will indeed become the one-world leader.[27] He will truly believe that he is God. He, himself, is corrupted to Satan's mindset that he is the ultimate power in the Universe.

Satan's Investment
The Beast will be amazing and dazzling as he will carry the investment of Satan's 6,000-year-old vision and plan to overturn God, who robbed him of his elevated position of "Star of the Morning," while in Heaven, only to be cast to the earth to crawl on his belly as a serpent.

His cunning plan is to shape the structure of world governments through secret societies, God-less philosophies, pseudo-churches, and mainline religions, so that at the coronation of his christ, he will rule over all. He will then, at some point, baptize the Antichrist with his "unholy spirit" and all power of his dark side will dwell in him.[28]

Surely, in keeping with his imitating way, he will mutter or pronounce to his minions, "This is my son in whom I am well pleased," in imitation of God and His Messiah. The Antichrist will come as teacher, friend, and the king of peace, and will bring a plan of a civilization of people who will surrender to him and worship him. What better place to make that plan etched in the minds of the people, than the seat of religion today—the Holy Place, in Holy Jerusalem.

The Dome of the Rock
While we have been taught that Christ cannot come until Solomon's Temple is rebuilt, we have overlooked that the Antichrist will come to a temple already built, and it will please the Muslims, who await their messiah—the Imam Mahdi, the Jews, who yet await their Messiah, and the ungrounded "Christians," who lack study.

Looking eastward to the site of the Holy of Holies.

I believe the Holy Place where the Antichrist will stand to declare himself God and simultaneously curse the God of

Heaven, will be the "Dome of the Rock."[29] It is the Holy Place for Islamics, who are the offspring of Ishmael, as well as the Jews, since the rock beneath the dome is where Abraham took his son Isaac to be a sacrifice, but where God provided the sacrifice, in a ram located in a nearby thicket. There, where the "Holy of Holies" was located in Solomon's Temple, where the Ark of the Covenant was located, must be the Holy Place that Daniel referred to.

Most any picture you will find of the "Mount of Zion," or Jerusalem, will show the gold-plated Dome of the Rock. This must be the most important, and violated place in the world, where the most Holy sites for Judaism, Christianity and Islam intersect.

HOW TO KNOW THE ANTICHRIST

Each person born has the right to a free will, or choice, as we have mentioned, it is the gift from God. Judas, who betrayed Jesus for thirty pieces of silver—had a choice. Even Lucifer had a choice to surrender to the Father, and humble himself, and so—the Antichrist, as well, must have the same choice. It does not follow our knowledge of God and His Creation, that any person would be born to be damned.

So, what can we know about him, who will precede the Second Advent of Christ? The prophet Daniel says that he will be unlike any who have come before him.[1] We can speculate about what that may mean, whether by his race, religion, appearance, quick rise to power, appeal to the people, background—it's anyone's guess. But we can know that in some obtuse (larger) way, he'll be different than those who have come before him.

A Mortal Wound
We can recognize him by what happens to him—a wound to his head that will be classified by medics, as a "mortal"

wound.[2] That means that he cannot live—as a result of it. My observation is that he may be kept on "life support" for a time, while a replacement can assume the position of his office. After the world has grieved sufficiently, (so an audience can be prepositioned), he will miraculously heal himself.[3] He will declare himself to be God and the leader of the world, who has come to bring peace to the world and economic stability. He will be the one whom the world has awaited,[4] but, he is not the Christ, he is the false christ, the one sent by Satan as his messiah. He will be a fraud, counterfeit, and an abomination to all that is Holy.

God's True Children will Recognize The Antichrist

Those who have been reborn of God's Spirit will recognize him in a heartbeat, in the same way as FBI agents are trained to spot counterfeit currency. They are trained in the handling and close scrutiny of legitimate cash, and when a counterfeit bill crosses their path—the "lights go off."

Sadly, there are many who claim to be Christians, but don't have the regular handling of His Presence to be able to tell the difference to discriminate between the real deal and a fake, when the fake is presented. That is why Jesus said that when they say to come here or go there to see Him—don't be tricked. You won't see the Messiah on TV,[5] but the only time you will see Him, is at His appearance in the clouds, at the Resurrection, which will be His Second Coming.[6]

Some Will Take the Mark

What will happen, as mentioned in the above paragraph, is the wholesale abandonment of an earlier commitment to Christ by many who become confused. When the tough times come with the rule of this sly and deceptive leader, droves of those who considered themselves Christian, will fall in line to take their oath of allegiance to the false-christ. They will be thinking and justifying it in their bosom, that they are do-ing the right thing; that since his deeds are miraculous—he surely is the Christ. And, since they can't feature living in this world without food, utilities, medical care, and the approval of those in their community, they will see no alternative, and will make the oath and take the brand of "Approved World Citizen."

The Mark of the Beast is a mark for damnation, just as cattle in a pen are marked with a red grease marker, for slaugh-ter, so is the Mark of the Beast a damning certification of the Second Death. The value to us here and now, is to know that there is no reversal, no forgiveness to taking the Mark of the Beast. Even if you are saved to the tenth power (if there is such a thing), you will be damned to Hell and your name will be erased from the Lamb's Book of Life![7] Don't let a "once saved, always saved" doctrine rob from you—Eternal Life.

A series of fictional books, *"The Left Behind"* series (The Mark, p. 353, 354, 355), teach a lie—that a Christian can take the Mark, "but not mean it," and no punishment will come to them. The Bible says something quite different.[8]

To those who are not buried in God's Word and are not well familiar with His teachings and commandments, and do not exercise worship and obedience through fellowship with Christ, it will be a "slam dunk" decision. Their response will be: "What choice do I have?"

We All Have a Choice
The choice we all have, all who live in those days, will be to:

1. Be party to Satan's plan to renounce Christ and the God of Heaven, and to turn against, shun, and turn in Christians (who will be labeled as enemies of the world),[9] to govern-

ment authorities. They will think that they have made the right decision and that peace will follow them many years. They will be the ones who will grieve at the sight of Christ's return,[10] for then they will recognize the grievous error they have made. They will curse God for their decision and grieve sorely as one grieves the loss of a first-born child.

2. To be forewarned and forearmed with the Word of God and the knowledge of His Return. This is critical, and it is the purpose of this book. God said that, "my people shall perish for a lack of knowledge." Holding and proclaiming the Truth of Christ's Return, is the thing that will make our witness and our preaching "valid," because when the Antichrist is revealed and Christ hasn't "raptured" Christians out of here, if our teaching of His Return is wrong, everything else will be assumed as wrong.

Saving the Chickens

Years ago, I was amazed at the outcome of a story out of England, where a large chicken processing plant had caught fire. Fire quickly enveloped the building, and several do-gooders rushed into the raging inferno to rescue as many chickens as they could. As a result, three people died in the rescue attempt.

I don't know what happened to the rescued chickens, but I imagine they were killed then for food, as was originally intended in the first place. So, three people died—saving chickens that were going to die anyway. I see a similar scenario with people who take the Mark of the Beast, in order to save their life, but in doing so, they lose their soul, and in a short time, lose their life anyway. Because they don't know Scripture and prophecy, they trade Eternal Life for eternal contempt—and they do so for the cheap price of temporary comfort and food. The purpose of this book and our Gospel

Tract printing ministry, is to prevent this kind of personal disaster.

The Mark of the Beast

I could refer you to a hundred books and thousands of Internet websites that teach only of the brand or mark that could be used to identify those who worship the Antichrist and who have forsaken the Christ of the Resurrection. The Bible says that the number of his name is 666 and that it can be calculated.[11]

In Hebrew, every letter has a numerical value, so when we calculate the values of each letter of a suspected name, when we get the right one, it will total 666. There are ministries today that are watch-dogging everyone who comes on the horizon as suspect, and they do so by "calculating the number of his name."

Additionally, the Bible says that the Mark will include a resemblance of him that seems to move.[12] That would suggest some type of hologram, or even with today's technology, it could very well be an LED Droid-type of device (sophisticated cell phone) that is implanted. We aren't going to suggest much past that because discoveries are coming to light so fast these days, we can only continue to monitor what might be used.

We know that there are two locations for the implant of the Mark: the right hand, or the forehead.[13] I can't foresee there being any "do over" as far as taking the Mark, as there is in golf. In other words, once you abandon and renounce Christ, in order to worship the Beast, you will be held in contempt for Eternity. As you study the Beast and his rule, you will see one thing that always will identify him—he is a copycat, and the Mark of the Beast is a perfect example. Jesus will write

His new name on the forehead of His followers and the name of Heaven, as well. He will "seal" His devoted followers unto Eternity, and so will the Antichrist.

Chapter 15

HOW CAN A CHRISTIAN PREPARE FOR THE GREAT TRIBULATION?

A good offense is the best defense.
Hold your friends close, your enemies closer.
Being forewarned is being forearmed.
"My people perish for a lack of knowledge."

That said, do you have any question how to prepare for the days ahead? While we can follow our gut, we really don't know when the Antichrist will come on the scene. He may have name recognition today while building alliances and political strengths, but the thing we must avoid at all costs— is labeling someone as the Antichrist until one or more Biblical proofs are made.

Those who are in His Word and are led by His Spirit will know when the Son of Perdition arrives. I would like even now to speculate as to who he is or what sector he may come from, but I must refrain as I encourage you to do, also. I am going to list some things for us all to do in preparation for the days ahead, whether they be twenty weeks or twenty years, before the onset of the Antichrist. We must live in Truth and we must leave Truth for those who follow.

1. Seek to know thoroughly the Big Picture of God's Creation, the first and second Advent of Christ.

2. Handle the real deal (fellowship in worship), the Messiah, and you will be able to spot the counterfeit. Pray in the Holy Spirit.

3. Become outspoken about the Blood of Christ to cleanse our soul of sin. Speak of the Resurrection unto Harvest. Hold Bible studies, Sunday school classes, and Internet teachings, because while the world is claiming that the end is now, you can teach that the end is near and lead souls to salvation.

4. Do as some denominations already teach, and prepare to live as long as possible, with your own water and food supplies, should there be a natural disaster. Practice the art of fasting. Abstain from food for one 24-hour period per month and spend time in prayer that would equal time normally spent in eating. Periods of fasting, two to three days would be a benefit, also. By doing that, you are able to subdue your stomach desires and increase your trust in the Lord's provision.

5. Seek the presence of the Holy Spirit as your Guide and Keeper, and walk in the faith He gives.

6. If that time should come in your lifetime, that you should be called forward to answer for the Name of Christ that you hold dear—DO NOT PREMEDITATE ON WHAT YOUR DEFENSE SHOULD BE, but rather, be yielded to the Holy Spirit and let His Words be your defense.[1]

7. Stock up on truthful literature that will tell the seeker about the time of trouble they are in and the only answer,

which is Christ.[2]

8. Be joyful in the Lord, knowing that it is appointed unto man once to die, and to die is gain. Don't be afraid. God will grant protection and strength and He will be glorified through you if you turn from temptation and resist evil.

9. For some reason, it seems that the Apostles stress that we especially not succumb to sexual sin. There are many sins, but this sin must be one that will cripple many in the last days after the restraint on sin is removed.

10. Realize that during a time of martial law, should we see it, the government will very possibly use trained clergy to pacify and subdue the masses. The clergy will intend to serve a righteous calling, but will unknowingly serve the Antichrist. They will use the Bible and most likely Romans 13, to convince citizens to submit, surrender, and serve the good of world citizens.

How Does the Non-Christian Prepare for the Great Tribulation?

1. I would hope that by now, you the reader—if unsaved or unsure of your salvation, would know what is the most important thing to do before the Great Tribulation. Yes, if you have read this far, it is clear that you have interest in life, and more specifically—Eternal Life. There is no one true formula, but at the same time—there is no other way than to surrender your heart and soul to the Son Who died on the Cross. This means becoming contrite, meek, and humble, repentant (God's Sorrow) and surrendered to His Lordship.

When you realize His love for you and that His death was on your behalf, then you can take Him as Lord. As you do, you will want to live for Him and sin no more. Then you can sing the words to the song: *"Because He lives, I can face tomorrow, because He lives, all fear is gone."* Welcome, as you join those who have also surrendered to Jesus Christ, and have had their names added to the Lamb's Book of Life.

2. Now, go to the above advice for Christians, and pick up from there. If you have not asked Christ to forgive and redeem you with His Blood—you are playing with dynamite and leaving poison lying around in the kitchen. Don't leave this paragraph until you have done business with the Lord. None of the information in this book is meaningful to you unless you have the Lord.

Many religions have altars where prayer and sacrifice is made to their god. The time and place where you give your heart to the Savior, can be your own altar.

I KNOW WHEN THE LORD IS COMING

Some time ago, I received an appeal letter from a missionary-evangelist whom I have supported. I call him brother, because of his apparent love for the Lord and his sacrifice in the mission field. The title of his letter was: I KNOW WHEN THE LORD IS COMING! This closely followed Harold Camping's failed prediction of His Coming on May 22, 2011, so like many others, I am sure, I became interested and read further.

I Received a New Understanding

As I read, I realized that among other things—he didn't know when the Lord was coming, however, as I researched my reply to him—a new understanding was opened to me. His beginning sentence was followed by a statement that explained that the Lord would come after the Gospel had been preached unto all the world, so he surmised that "the Lord is waiting on us to evangelize the world so He could return." I don't believe that the Lord waits on any man and I replied such to him.

Like so many things we have heard from teachers and preachers, these words didn't match the things I have read, so I thought it a good time to revisit Matthew 24. A verse of Scripture where Jesus told the disciples not to meditate or give any thought to the defense we might give on account of His Name when brought before the magistrates, weighed heavily on my mind for some reason. I searched Matthew hard for that verse but couldn't see it, so I went to Mark 13 and it jumped out at me.

Something else jumped out at me as I read in the following verses: *"9. But take heed to yourselves: for they shall deliver you up to councils; and in the synagogues ye shall be beaten: and ye shall be brought before rulers and kings for my sake, for a testimony against them. 10. And the gospel must first be published among all nations. 11. But when they deliver you up, take no thought beforehand what ye shall speak, neither do ye premeditate: but whatsoever shall be given you in that hour, that speak ye: for it is not ye that speak, but the Holy Ghost."*

Between the two verses I was looking for was the verse used by my evangelist-friend, that the Gospel shall be preached unto all the world. I wasn't looking for that verse, so I was surprised to see it there. It seemed that, that verse was misplaced or out of context. Until this day, I guess I just "read over it," not giving any thought to its position (we do that often when we don't really understand, we just read words, not meaning).

A Sensational Murder Trial
At that particular time, in the summer of 2011, the murder trial of a young Florida mother who was charged in the murder of her toddler daughter had the nation all abuzz. Because of the media attention and fascination by the people, perhaps because it was a death-penalty case with murder, lies,

and bizarre lifestyles, many Florida residents slept in line the night before to get tickets to the trial. That's when it all fell into place for me. Jesus knew well the hatred that will be placed against those who claim His Name for themselves.

Christianity will be synonymous with world traitor and enemy of "Our Beloved Beast," and those taken captive, tortured, and beaten will be hauled up before the courts of the land to "give account of their faith in Jesus the Christ." That account most likely will grant their death sentence and the people will love it as they say, "finally—those Christians will get what they deserve!"

They will view the "questioning" on their iPad or Droid device, as others strain in little crowds to see it for themselves. The news venues will splash their pages and airwaves with trial results, words of defense, and most likely, so will executions, because it will seemingly serve the agenda of the Antichrist, as it will also feed the appetite of the "world citizens."

The words spoken by the Holy Ghost will infuriate those who have always hated Him, but will woo others, who have rejected the Mark of the Beast, but who haven't yet taken Christ. With a heart tendered by Him and by the events of the day, they will manifest revival.

The Gospel Preached in all Nations

Now we can see the reason Jesus spoke to us, to *"take no thought beforehand what ye shall speak, neither do ye premeditate:"* because the Holy Spirit will speak through us as His Divine Instrument, and there, brothers and sisters, you will have the the Gospel preached unto all nations and in their own tongue!

The message will be pure and anointed because it will be from the Holy Ghost of God. Two things will then happen: the powerful Gospel message from God Himself will ring true to those not yet bearing the Mark of the Beast and many of them will say: "That's what I am looking for—the Truth! That is the answer for me—I have rejected Christ for years, but I can see that this other guy is not the Christ, but an impostor. Now, I have but one choice and while it will be my death—it will be my life also."

And the great revival at the "end of time" that we have always expected, will ensue. While the trials will be meant to sway the undecided, it will! It will sway them both ways as the goats are marked for doom and sheep marked for reward. Those martyred for His Name's sake will also give strength to those living without purpose. For sure, this is a time when the Holy Spirit will not be "taken out" as we have been taught, but to the contrary, He will be speaking through His beloved children, wonderful words of Love, Forgiveness, Redemption, and of a soon resurrection unto Everlasting Life.

The Christians who have gone underground will see that revival has come and they, too, will be preaching under the power and unction of the Holy Ghost. I doubt that you will see what we label today as "confessions of faith" or "confirmations," or "baptisms," as a key to salvation, but because the stakes will be high, those new converts will be changed from the inside out, "born again," "surrendered," and, Redeemed by the Blood. They will be filled with the Holy Ghost, giving them strength and power to testify of His Grace in a hostile environment, and as well, they will be given sufficient Grace to suffer if called to.

THE DARK DAYS OF THE GREAT TRIBULATION

A nyone who has served the Lord boldly, has felt Satan's scorn. I have, and on multiple occasions. It is hard, but it is good, in that you walk in the "valley of the shadow of death," and the victory is yours because of the Lord. The "good" part of such battles, is the adrenalin rush of the battle and the victory. I have been in that valley, both in my home church and in the trenches fighting for souls, at home and in the mountains of Haiti. The force of darkness is awesome, but the overcoming Light is so much more. While I have had demon-possessed people come at me and curse me in demonic gibberish, I just grab the horn of God's Throne and rebuke the powers of darkness until they wither and whine away into the night.

In the periods of "spiritual peace," spiritual warriors long for the fight, because they know the intoxication of fierce battle, when you are on the winning side. During the Great Tribulation, the battle for souls will be intense. You see, while many, at first, will fall in line to worship the Beast and take the Mark of a proper world-citizen, but—there will also be a certain element who won't "buy into it."

They will be non-conformists, who don't like anyone telling them what to do, those who are not sticklers for doing what the law requires, and even "occupiers" who don't like the establishment. There will be pleas and even commands to fall in line or face punishment, but that will make them more resistant, because truth is more important to them than comfort.

The Two Witnesses

As persecution of those who fail to worship the Beast intensifies, so does the greatest revival of all times.[1] Underground churches will spring up and the people who have found the faith to believe, faith they always desired, but could never muster, will be emboldened with every message that comes from Jerusalem where the Antichrist will rule from.

There, two witnesses of God will prophesy in the streets of Jerusalem (the Holy City) and bring curses from Heaven that will hit directly in the kingdom of the Antichrist, and the people who worship him will be furious with God.[2] Many will try to kill the witnesses, but God will slay them with His Word. Finally, the Antichrist does kill them and they are left to lie dead in the streets for three and one-half days, as the world watches and celebrates their death. Their presence is marked by the abomination of desolation (the start of the Great Tribulation, and, ends at the Second Coming of Christ.

It will be like Christmas in reverse, for the world will celebrate the death of God's anointed witnesses, by a season of gift-giving and feasts; in the same way we celebrate the Birth of God's Son at Christmas time. It is hard to tell for sure, but it seems like resurrection of the two witnesses coincides with the coming of Christ when the other saints of God also rise to meet Him in the air. It would make the most sense and understanding that they rise, as well as other saints who have died, at Christ's Return—otherwise another installment to the Resurrection must be numbered. Those witnesses may be Elijah and Enoch, since neither one died but were "translated" to Heaven (Go directly to Heaven, bypass death). Many teachers believe this because *"it is appointed unto men once to die..."*[3]

The celebration of the death of the two witnesses turns sour indeed, when the last trump sounds and there is a shout in Heaven announcing the end of the age of mercy. The sudden realization that it was not Christ that the proper New World citizens worshiped, but an impostor, will turn a holiday into the greatest personal disaster of all time.

They will grieve and curse God for their error[4] when they realize that they have been left behind and stand squarely on the wrong side of the Almighty. There is a silence in Heaven for the period of an half-hour, like the eye of a category 5 hurricane. The damned will no doubt be stunned after seeing the clouds roll away like a scroll, while at the same time, all Heaven breaks out in a chorus of the Four-fold Hallelujahs,[5] as Christ Himself comes to receive His Bride.

While perhaps taking a short time, His Coming and the Resurrection will be Victorious with a capital V, and the ensuing silence will most likely—be deafening. Silence—in itself— will be a "cruel and unusual" punishment, like standing on a gallows floor with hands and legs bound, neck-tie tight and in place, as moments pass—each seeming like hours, knowing that the floor will soon transfer your weight to the rope around your neck.

But, the silence differs from the wait at the gallows, because at least the gallows would bring an end to suffering—death would be welcomed. Death and its finality would not be found for those left; men will cry for the mountains to fall on them[6]—so their misery will have an end, but there will be no one to hear their prayer, since the windows of Heaven are now shut.[7]

That interlude of an half hour in Heaven leaves the assumption that it is on earth as it is in Heaven. It seems that this is another "offset moment," because while those who remain on earth, become aware of the Wrath to come; the Redeemed need the time for themselves to come to their senses. The power to erase from their mind—the taint and curse of sin, leaving purity and righteousness in its place, has come upon them. The power that will come from the Resurrection will be the exhilaration that will leave them breathless. Maybe that will account for the half hour of silence in Heaven, just following Christ's Return and just prior to God's Wrath to be poured out upon the ungodly. I can see it now, and as I think about it for a moment, I am convinced that when the power of God changes our nature from corruptible to incorruptible, and our bodies from mortal to immortal, it's going to take more than a couple moments to transition.

Chapter

18

THE SECOND COMING
OF CHRIST—THE DAY
OF JUDGMENT

Brought into confusion, concerning Christ's Return, is the use of two terms: The Day of Jesus Christ and The Day of the Lord. The reason for confusion, is because they are the same day, but at different times of the day, and of different purposes. For example: The Time of Jacob's Trouble, and the time of the Great Tribulation occur during

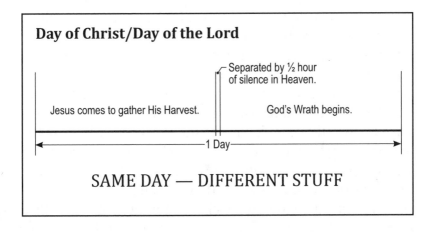

Day of Christ/Day of the Lord

⌐ Separated by ½ hour
of silence in Heaven.

Jesus comes to gather His Harvest.   God's Wrath begins.

←————————————1 Day————————————→

SAME DAY — DIFFERENT STUFF

the same last seven years of this earth, but one is within the other and is of different purpose. Both are of Satan: The installment of the Antichrist before the time of Jacob's Trouble, and his wrath against God's people, manifested through the Great Tribulation, three and one half years after the signing of the Covenant of Peace, which marks Jacob's Trouble.

If you are keeping score, add this to the several OFFSET DEVICES that are so evident and prevalent after we realize that Satan is a copycat and creates nothing. The coming of his christ and his wrath against God's own, appears to be his special design, but it is not. He is an imitator of God, he knows from Scripture what God is going to do.

The Day of Jesus Christ

This day, when the Father Who sits on the Throne, tells Jesus to go and "bring My children home," is the day referred to as the Blessed Hope. It is the time of all times and the pinnacle of all that is, and it will be the most spectacular, wonderful, as well as terrible, event we can imagine.

First, will be the sounding of the Last Trump of God, followed by a tremendous shout in Heaven. The shout is crashing, and crushing, as it ends the days of Mercy and Grace for this earth. This victorious moment is likened unto the falling into the earth, of the walls of the city of Jericho, following the last trumpet and the great shout by all the people. The shout can be likened to the report of a rifle shot, once the trigger is pulled, things happen quickly and they can't be rescinded. Like the bullet leaving the barrel, so is Christ's presence known. It is known first by the sign of the Savior in the sky, then immediately, the clouds roll away as a scroll and Jesus appears in the sky—the Hope of Glory achieved. The last time He came into town, He was riding a donkey, symbolizing the surrendered, meek servant, but this time it's a different story. The beautiful, powerful white horse is one of Victory and Dominance. He comes from on high and He has come for those who are looking for His Return.[1]

He comes also—as a thief in the night,[2] but not as a thief for the Redeemed, because they will be anticipating His Return[3] and because they are of "light." But for those who are of darkness, He will come and rob them of all that they have trusted in. He won't take from them that which is theirs, but instead, He will ensure that they get to keep what they have sought: Their beloved Antichrist, their One-World system, security, their hatred for God, and their rejection of Truth. What He will take from them, is what they wanted to be rid of anyway—the Christians, and the Righteousness they brought to the world. Then the Truth that they have rejected, will crush them by its illumination at His Return.

At His Return, all who went to their death as saints of God, will rise to meet Him in the air,[4] as well as those who are yet alive on the earth, who will join them for the Harvest of Souls. At the same time, those who are dead also, but who are dead to Christ are also Resurrected[5]—but they don't rise above the earth, they have their feet planted on the sod of the earth as they join the other damned in realizing their worst dream has come true.

The Day of the Lord
Same day, different stuff, as they say. Yes, as the Christ has come and like a bullet, or more like lightning, Jesus circles the earth, going from the east to the west,[6] gathering His Own, and in a moment, or more like the "twinkling of an eye," the Harvest unto Resurrection is completed.

It was very noisy and full of activity for an instant, and now— all is quiet[7], very, very quiet: The Day of the Lord is very near. Like the words penned by Julia Ward Howe in 1856, *Mine eyes have seen the glory of the coming of the Lord. He has trampl'd out the vintage where the grapes of wrath are stored.*

So now that the focus of the Day of Jesus Christ has been completed, the day wears on for those who remain on the earth, as The Day of the Lord begins and lasts for several days. But before it begins, there is an "offset" to the unbelievable joy and exhilaration by the Redeemed at the promised return of Jesus, their Messiah. That offset comes during the half-hour of silence when the damned realize the folly of their ignorance and that now they will become the target of a very angry and vengeful God. They have seen His judgments and now, knowing how they treated the Children of God, the knowledge of all of what is due them, falls on them like something worse than the pall of death. They will scream, cry, wail, and curse the day of their birth,[8] curse the God of Heaven and curse each other. They will cry for the mountains to fall on them so that they might be excused from the Wrath, but they will not be excused.

Why We Must Know of These Things

We must know of the Day of Jesus Christ and, as well, the Day of The Lord, so we can be rightfully prepared. We must know so we can prepare our children and parents, our neighbors and friends. We must know so we are properly prepared with our lamps trimmed and full of oil, and our robes white, without soiling. Then, when the Trump is heard and the Shout felt, there won't be any last minute details to attend—we will be properly prepared for the Grand Finale!

GOD'S WRATH AND THE AFTERMATH

My son-in-law innocently planned to discard some old gasoline that he had in a large shallow drain pan. As he poured the gas slowly into a burn barrel that he thought was cold, it flashed up and fire was everywhere. It sloshed onto his shorts and legs, and for some time, he was fighting for his life. That horrible accident reminded me of the seven vial judgment that follows the Great Tribulation. After the one-half hour of silence, the Wrath of God, that has been held back by centuries of long-suffering, starts to slosh from the vials, which are more like "lavers" (very shallow pans used to catch the blood of sacrificed animals in Old Testament worship) and the calm on earth quickly turns to Hell as the damned begin a fight for their lives—a fight they won't win. The fire falls and the earth is an ugly place to be for thirty days, according to Daniel's prophecy and the Book of Revelation. That thirty day time of Wrath appears to be extended another forty-five days, as God's Wrath is greater than earlier thought.[1] But wait, it's time for the Son to come with His army and finish what the Father started.

Meanwhile, in Heaven

The picture that has been painted for us in Revelation, about
the time of God's Wrath, is one that is so horrible—we can
scarcely take it in. There is a reason for that! Remember back
at the first of this book, we talked about the Law of Opposition? Now is a good time to savor the effects of that law, that
is—if you are one of the Meek, Called by His Name, Bought
by His Blood, Delivered from Perdition, Sealed as His Own—
or simply that your name has been written in the Lamb's
Book of Life.

After you see what happens simultaneously on earth and in
Heaven, immediately following the Resurrection at Christ's
Return—I must ask you, "Why would you from this point forward, do anything that does not enhance God's Kingdom and
your love and worship of the Savior?"

You see: Now that the windows of Heaven are closed for this
"past earth and the age of satanic rule," the activities of life
are more pronounced and intense because they have been
divided by the poles that draw them: evil to evil, righteousness to righteousness. The same for reward and punishment.
Presently on earth, we find good and bad, right and wrong,
sweet and sour—side by side. If I could right now, I would
transport you to Haiti with me, and there, we would bask
in delightful fragrance—in one breath, and nearly gag in the
next. Yes, we live in an environment of choice and the accom-
paniments to choice are a mixed bag.

When the Four Hallelujahs ring out—all that changes. There
is a lot going on for sure, both in Heaven, on earth and in
the air above the earth. It can't be told in one sentence, or
one paragraph, even one chapter. In Revelation 11, we see
the first mention of His Return in verse 15. Verses following
that and even chapters later, we are still reading about the

aspects of that wonderful event.

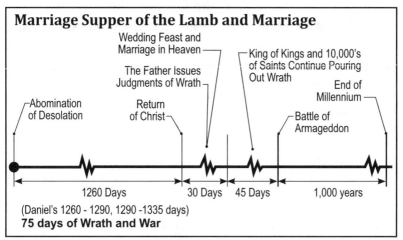

The Marriage Supper

In Matthew 22, we hear the first about a wedding feast, as told by Jesus in a parable, and that is the only mention of it until Revelation 19. There, we are told about the loud voice in Heaven as a great multitude pronounce the Hallelujah Declaration, either in song or strong statement, then the angels rejoice and prepare the Supper.

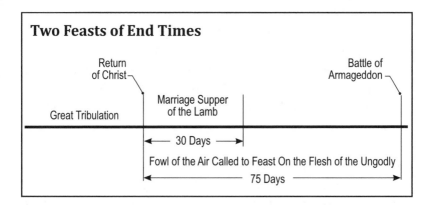

There are actually two suppers occurring at this time, and again—we see an offset-action while the Redeemed feast in

Heaven with the Lamb, while on earth, the birds of the earth are gorging themselves on the flesh of those who have rejected Christ.[2] While the Redeemed drink the best wedding wine, the damned are served the wine tread from the grapes of wrath. The Law of Opposition can't be more strongly illustrated than in this scene.

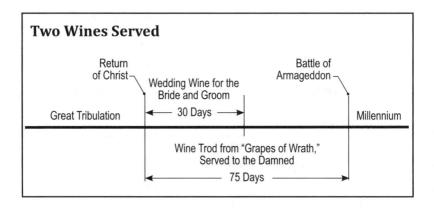

Family Reunion

The Bible teaches of several types of feasts that were and are yet today observed by many. God designed food and the fellowship that comes with eating together with friends and family. How often do we grab some friends or family members and go out to eat, or "do lunch" together? What would be a gathering, without something to eat? The Marriage Supper will be all that and much more. There will be rejoicing with those who will share Eternity together. The bond with the Lord Jesus will be strengthened by this intimate fellowship.

I suppose that there will be stories and mysteries revealed as the Bride gasps at every word of the Bridegroom, and at the miracle of everything that has just happened. The food and wine will nurture and heal those who have been resting in the dust of the earth and those who experienced the Great

Tribulation and the suffering and testing of men's souls. The release of worry and care will equal the suffering and dread of those yet on earth—who did not hearken to the call of repentance and surrender at the Cross of Calvary.

In the classic book, *"A Tale of Two Cities,"* by Charles Dickens, we find words that stick with us even today: "It was the best of times, it was the worst of times." This accurately describes the days to come, when Jesus punctuates life and ends the world as we know it now—at His Return.

The Holy Sabbath: The Last Election Cycle
Christians are most confused about the time that has been ordained by the Father, for the Son to rule the earth, and I have to ask why? Remember one of the "understanding structures" we started this project with—learning how to fly? And to fly, we have to build an aircraft using principles of flight that are well-tested.

If the prophecy craft isn't of the design of proper weight and balance, all your work and planning is for naught, because before you get to the test-flight stage—things don't fit together so well. That's what happens when you start following man's teachings about the timing of things; when you get to the end—you have more hard questions and less answers than when you began.

There is a new earth coming, that is structured to the form and function of Christ's Reign of a thousand years. It comes about, following the "two feasts," the Marriage Feast and the Wrath of God (the bird feast). In my time of pre-Tribulation Rapture believing, I gave little thought to the Millennium of Christ. It seemed unimportant to me, since I believed that I would be in Heaven and everything else would fall into place. Then after the scales literally fell off my eyes and I began to understand the Resurrection, I was asked by several people, about the Millennium. My response was, "It is coming together, but I have my hands full sorting out and teaching the Tribulation, and that was my largest concern." Furthermore, it didn't seem that there was much teaching in the Bible about the Millennium, so I just read over some gold nuggets, because I didn't have a place to put the pieces. What has happened since, is that the Millennium explains itself—in understanding, just like building an airplane or assembling a 1,000 piece puzzle. When you only have a few pieces left— they kind of jump in place.

THE "WHY" OF IT

I don't know if now is the time to stop and gather our senses, or if we should have paused for a break before starting this chapter. What we are learning from the puzzle pieces of Scripture are beyond our limits of reason. What we have seen in our lifetime, is sun up, then sun down; year in, year out. And probably most of us have seen one century change, and it has been like that for many generations. When we talk about destructions and creations of the earth—we don't have any frame of reference. We have the Biblical record to go by, but we don't even know anyone who has seen something really big—like the Great Flood. Many people don't even believe it happened, so when we study the things that were told to us, that will happen, we are going to need to generate some very large faith. To imagine Jesus ruling over the world from the Temple Mount in Jerusalem and His martyred saints over the nations and cities—it takes a real step of faith. Then to imagine that those living on the earth will live for one thousand years—it almost seems incredulous.

What makes it believable, is the fulfilled prophecy of past times and the ease of which the puzzle of life does go together. So on one hand, it does take a lot of faith to believe that we are on the edge of this "world" passing from us, as another world comes before us. When you study the words of prophecy and align them with the way the world is heading now—it almost doesn't require faith at all, because the New World Order and the platform for the rule of the Antichrist that we see today, makes more sense and is more plausible than anything else at this point.

The things we are going to talk about, now that we have had a breather, are the "most-probable" aspects of the world under the Millennial Reign of Christ.

Heaven on Earth

When we started this journey, you and I, we read and read deeply, the first five verses of the Bible, then we understood that contrary to our Sunday school lessons, Heaven for Eternity will reside right here on this earth.[1]

But first, a "Heavenly" time on earth must pass: The Millennial Reign of Christ. Probably the first question that Christians have about this coming time is: "What's the purpose? We have lived life and survived the test, does this mean that we have to do it all over again?"

For the answer, first we look at the nature of God, then do some simple math.

1. Of His nature, we know that He is just and fair in all things. He wants those who are devoted to Him to praise and worship Him, by their own volition. Likewise He wants those who have rejected Him and who have worked evil against Him, to exalt and declare Him Lord; also by their own volition, even though they stand condemned. That way, no one can with legitimacy, blame God for their fate.

2. The math of it: For some reason of Creation, seven has spe-

cial strength and is known as God's perfect number. When this world was created at Eden (2nd world), God rested on the seventh day (Sabbath) as a completion of perfection. He labored for six days, rested on the seventh and the week was complete.

Peter reminded us that to God, a day is as a thousand years and a thousand years is as a day.[2] It's not as though God can't tell the difference, but more like in "symbolic representation." We know that roughly, 6,000 years have passed since the creation of Adam and Eve. Bible scholars suggest that Adam and Eve lived as long as one hundred-twenty years in the Garden of Eden before the forbidden fruit was tasted.

Many scholars believe that 6,000 years will have been completed between the years 2008 and 2017. We just don't have an accurate calendar for that much time, but the best guess is somewhere in that time frame—the time that was given to Satan as "god of this world" will come to an end. With that said, we can trust that the Sabbath is soon to come.

It is simple math. 6 + 1 = 7. Now: for the "changing of the guard," there will necessarily come a time of handing over the reigns of leadership, and that doesn't come without a certain amount of violence and wrest (with force, taking leadership from its present holder). Remember that Satan hates God and wants to be God. He thinks that by destroying God's Chosen people and the Elect, God will have nowhere to go. The battle has been chosen long ago and will commence—shortly.

The transition between Satan's 6,000 year reign and Christ's 1,000 year reign, takes seven years and that seven years is represented by the Time of Jacob's Trouble. The last half of that seven year time is the Great Tribulation.

Now—the Purpose

From the time Lucifer was a chosen angel in God's Diadem, until now, he feels superior to God. He is the essence of PRIDE. He is concentrated, undiluted, compressed, and liquefied PRIDE. It wouldn't be enough for God to blast him to Hell and just say, ah—to Hell with him and good riddance. God, in His fair and just Righteousness, must settle the issue for all time. He does that with the Millennial Reign of His Son, Jesus. By this new rule on earth, Righteousness and Holiness directs the path of man to do His work and to raise up a people who grow under the admonition of The Lord, as opposed to the perversion and deception of evil, as was experienced in the first 6,000 years.

Satan Is Loosed

Then, as we read again in Revelation 20, Satan must be loosed for a little season. Christians have never understood that before—Why must he be loosed for a little season, they ask? So he can deceive the nations! Why, again they ask? So God's purpose can be achieved—and that is to vex Satan and to put to end the pride essence that has driven him. God's Word doesn't say that he is victorious or defeated, in deceiving those born under the Millennial Reign, but it must be that he finds severe rejection. This causes him to go "in" to the four quarters of the earth, Gog and Magog, to "gather them

Satan loosed for "a little season"

Great Tribulation	75 Days of Wrath	Millennium Reign of Christ		Unknown Little Season of Deception
			?	?
		Gleanings Which Completes First Resurrection		

together." *"And they went up on the breadth of the earth..."* (Revelation 20:8,9). Gog refers to a ruler and Magog, a place, or people.

He will deceive his minions once more, into thinking that they could actually kill God and His saints who were camped about the Holy City, Jerusalem. And just like the Ammorites, Hittites, and those of Mt. Seir, who came against King Jehoshaphat and Judah[3], the Lord routed them with a "fog of confusion" and they killed each other, to the last one. So will the armies of Satan, who come against the Holy City, it's saints and King, be slaughtered to the last one, in the great battle known as the Battle of Gog and Magog, or the final conflict (since there is no battle at all), only destruction by the Lord, as He sends fire from Heaven.[4]

The damned and their leader will finally have the wind completely taken out of them and then the Judgment takes place immediately. There and then is when every knee shall bow and every tongue confess (even Satan's) that Jesus is Lord. They do that in uncontested surrender, just as Japan's Foreign Minister Mamoru Shigemitsu and General Yoshijiro Umezu, Chief of the Army General Staff, signed an unconditional surrender to the United States, 2 Sept. 1945.

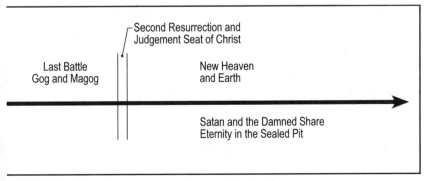

The purpose of the Millennial Reign has escaped us for these many years and finally, it makes sense, but now let's see what it will look like.

What Will the Millennium Look Like for the Redeemed?
What we know for sure—is very little, but from what we know, we can assume much. We know that:
1. The wolf will lie beside the lamb.[5]
The food chain will be altered, very likely our diet will strictly be vegetarian.
Today's predators will undergo a transformation that comes with the new earth, and become vegetarians also.
Fear of animals evaporates.
2. That we will beat our weapons into plowshares.[6]
Our focus will be in crop production.
Recycling of earth's resources will take full swing, as tanks, planes, and rifles will be forged into tractors, plows and combines (there will be work to do).
Farming will be a joy because weather won't be such an issue, since most likely the earth will be restored to the Antediluvian state and pests such as weevils and blight will be non-existent since the curse will have been lifted.
Crops will be watered nightly by heavy dews.
3. That the Redeemed will live for a thousand years.[7]
The Antediluvian state (moisture of earth held in atmosphere, creating very high density altitude, which is high pressure oxygen level) enables us to live for 1,000 years, be very healthy and able to run and work hard without tiring.
4. That Jesus will be the King of kings.[8]
This was God's wish from the beginning, to be man's King, but we wanted an earthly king and so God let us have the desires of our heart.[9]
There will be no more election cycles or dirty politics. We will have a benevolent and righteous King.

5. Those martyred during the Tribulation will rule the nations.[10]

The people born into Christ's one-world system will have the benefit of serving under those who God chose and who also chose Him. They will teach God's law and rule under His law.

6. That the Redeemed who inherit the earth will give birth to those who will inhabit the earth, though the Redeemed will not marry and give in marriage as we do today, because the marriage that is Holy, is between the Bride and Christ. There will not be temptation under the King of kings, nor perversion, so when the Tempter is loosed for a little season, the wisdom of Godly teachers and parents will expose Satan for the fool he truly is. Men will be "men" and women will be "women." Yea! Just as in the Garden of Eden, when God gave man a suitable companion (woman) and not a wife.

7. That our bodies will be "Glorified."[11]

Our corruptible flesh will be exchanged for incorruptible and we will be "restored." What God made in His image, will be our likeness. If we were scarred, maimed, circumcised, mutilated, dismembered, or if we were born effeminate, butch, deformed, or mentally challenged in any way in life before, then just as this earth was, we too, will be restored to "our former glory" as designed in the Garden of Eden. This alone should bring everyone to their knees in repentance. Who would not sell all they own to buy such a body? Who would find pleasure in sin, knowing that it would cost them God's best?

What We Don't Know About the Millennium

Since there will be birthing and children to raise, what about marriage? Now that the Redeemed will be the Bride to the Groom King, the Redeemed will not marry or give in marriage, but certainly, will then receive the mate that He gives, just as Adam received Eve as His gift to him. It is interesting that God didn't give Adam a wife, but a companion, a woman. Most of us would assume that there would be marriage, but that, as other questions we might have, are a moot point right now. It is good for us to view and dream of life under the King of kings and to know that worship will be better than Christians of today can only dream of.

While I, and most believers I know, have a dim understanding of Heaven on Earth, which is the Heaven to come, I think its understanding has been kept from us until now; otherwise, many would seek salvation solely for the "inherit effects" and not for the purpose of loving God. We love God for who He is, we also love Him because it is best for us. Loving Him just for the goodies is shallow love that won't carry us through the fire.

The Close of the Millennium

At the end of the thousand years, the "rest of the dead" will be raised.[12] They are the ones we called group three, in chapter nine. These are the folks who lived on the earth, but for some unknown reason, were unable to either choose or reject Christ. I would imagine there would be a time of orientation so they will know of Satan's rule on earth, of the Great Tribulation, Christ's Return, and the General Resurrection, which their Resurrection is the final part of. When they see and hear Christ on the Throne and know the story, they then will be asked to choose.

Then Satan will be released from his prison and he will be red-hot mad, soaked in venomous hatred for Jesus and all that is Holy, because of his imprisonment. He will go out to deceive the nations, but I think he will have a very bad showing and shame will consume him. Not missing a beat, he takes a further step: like a "Hail Mary pass" in a game he is losing and has no chance of winning, where he isn't going to be taken alive, he deceives those in bondage, into thinking together—they can kill God and be done with it.

The Final Earth: Eternal Heaven, On Earth
All who are defeated at the final conflict of Gog and Magog, will stand before the Judge and the books read aloud. Those who are Redeemed have an Advocate, (Jesus) who steps in and excuses them from the proceedings, saying, "These stand here guiltless, for I died on their behalf. They are signed, sealed and delivered from these proceedings." Following the sentencing of the Damned, to exile in outer darkness, the new Heaven and Earth comes down. The earth was burned, along with the works of man, during the Judgment time, and now it is God's newest finished Creation.

Heaven on Earth is large indeed: fifteen-hundred miles in every direction[13] and a new name which will glorify it. A wonderful description of Heaven is found in Revelation 21 and 22. Servants of the Most High will attend Him. There will be no Temple, because both the Father and the Lamb are the Temple. They whose names are written in the Lamb's Book of Life will come in and out of the gates, which never are closed, and it will resemble in many ways, the Garden of Eden.

Again, much can be imagined about Heaven, but probably the most valuable knowledge we can gain from the vivid description, is that it is a very physical place where sensory overload could occur. Saints and kings alike, will come and go through the gates of the Holy Jerusalem; there will be food to eat and that is physical.

I have no doubt about enjoying Heaven. I know the things that God likes, because I see them heavily in Creation. He won't stop liking these things, nor creating them and thus will greatly infuse them into His Eternal Heaven.

The End of the Puzzle

Perhaps it has been the things in the world today that brought you to try finding the answers to your personal spiritual puzzle, or maybe you can't label the reason for your searching, but without a doubt—questions that have come to you—are ordained of God. He wants you to draw unto Him. If you were perfect, or nearly so, you would have been translated to Heaven like Elijah or Enoch, but since you aren't, He has left you here and given many opportunities for you to conform to His image, and He is not done with you yet. He desires that, should you be tested in such a way as is most difficult, you would give honor and glory to His Name, and Satan would be foiled. Our desire should not be the easy-soft way, but as Peter desired, *"That I may know him...and the fellowship of his sufferings..."*[14]

Then, He would be proud to have you serve as a governor or king in the earth to come, when He reigns as King of kings. The problem with us, is that most of us are deceived into thinking we are "approved" or Born Again. Churches, anxious to fill their rolls and bolster their numbers, present members to the congregations, well before the heart has changed. So, like the Christian joke goes, "because they live in a garage, they think themselves to be a car."

Most other people are convinced that they are Christians too, or at least have "made their peace with God." The coming period of Tribulation will separate the real-deal from the wannabe. Our protection against becoming swallowed by the greatest scam the world has ever, or ever will know, is to "handle the genuine article," and know Him intimately. Otherwise, we might not spot the counterfeit, until we become completely blinded. The Prophecy Puzzle is completed when we place ourselves in His Hands, by repentance and through faith.

The purpose of this book is to present the Big Picture of Creation, the understanding of spiritual laws, and a piece-by-piece assembly of how the end of this world will come about. We do this so if this week, this year, in our lifetime, or in our children's lifetime, we who are God's plan, can go into it, fully knowing what to expect and how to prepare. We have to live our lives as though we may never see the revelation of the Antichrist, and at the same time, we must live and teach as though it is only months way. The balance, is that of adopting a strategy of being a sojourner—just passing through. We have to hold the things of this life loosely, just as we would a hand crank on an antique tractor, not wrapping our thumb around it, so when it lights up, it doesn't light us up as well.

Therefore, keeping our eye on the prize, we run the race of love and obedience and in the fear of God. May He be praised by this reading. Amen

Post Script

Like I said at the start of this book, we didn't intend to even try to answer all the questions you may have, and even if we were able, it wouldn't be right. God wants you to search the answers by going to His Word and in prayer—earnestly seek to know Him, and you can only do that by letting Him speak to you through His Word.

So, now that you have in this book a common-sense approach to understanding more about God and the evil one, Satan, the many details of the Days of the End Times come together with study. The clearest discourse by Jesus about the signs of His Return and of the end of time, came when the disciples asked Him what to expect. They had just entered the Mount Of Olives, so the conversation is referred to as the Olivette Discourse. Like puzzle pieces found by different manufacturers, as we discussed, some words will differ, some will be omitted, but by comparing and studying each, you will find remarkable clarity.

John must have been absent from the gathering, because he records nothing of the Olivette Discourse. The others you should read and compare: Matthew 24, Mark 13, and Luke 21.

The Book of Daniel is good for deep study, but chapters 7-12 offer the most information to end time prophecy. I Thessalonians, II Thessalonians, I Corinthians 15, and the Book of Jude are also helpful. Ezekiel 37, 40, and of course—Revelation, have a wealth of insight. There are snippets and single verses in the most obscure places, so keep your face in the Book.

We started out thinking that we would be able to introduce items like: The Great Tribulation, then God's Wrath, and on to the Millennial Reign of Christ in separate areas, unlike the Bible, where nothing is in order or separate. Then, we discovered that it is impossible to talk about one thing without getting involved in another, because it is all tied together. There is wonderful agreement in this tapestry of prophecy. Among the things that warm my soul, are the Marriage Supper and Wedding. Just as a bride of today takes the name of her husband, so will the Bride of Christ when He writes on the forehead, the new name of Christ. It will be a wedding and bonding which will seal forever, Jesus—with His Saints. You will see also, when you read in Revelation 2 and 3, (message to the seven churches) the rewards promised to those who overcome sin, and those rewards will be granted at the Marriage and days to follow. Study those promises and dwell on the privilege and honor He will bestow, once the time comes. After you study the things He has planned for His Redeemed, the bit of suffering we might incur, will be such a small price to pay for the privilege of loving and serving Him for endless ages.

The days at the end are scary to most people. They are afraid to know what will come, because it may bring discomfort. For decades, I have heard people comment about how blessed the people of America are, and as I have traveled back and forth from Haiti so many times in the past thirty years, I see how a people who have so little of the luxuries of this world—have so much that should be desired. On the other hand, I see a people who have so much of the luxuries, but miss the joy of life. Then, I say to myself, "Are we truly blessed by so much, or will our physical wealth be the thing that causes our destruction?" I think the latter must be the case. When the rich and satiated have to go without—they will cave in to their stomach cravings; they won't be able to survive on scraps and in most cases, I am afraid they will be snared into a damnable trap, thereby missing the things promised by the Lord to those who overcome sin.

Study and find thyself approved. Desire not to just get by (spiritually), but to overcome and trample over the Liar and Thief. Speak the truth boldly so others will find the way and when He comes, He will find you well and you family healthy and well fed (Matthew 25). Feel free to contact us with questions or help in your personal ministry. We would like to supply you with up-to-date tracts, letters and magazines that will enable you to minister to your family and friends, so write us today and request sample tracts, or to be put on our mailing list. We charge for nothing, but provide as the Lord gives us the means. By that, we would welcome you to join others of this Society to help pass the Good Word of the Lord to the world who so desperately need to know of Jesus and of His Blood.

Tom Buttram

Gospel Tract Society, Inc.
POB 1118
Independence MO 64050

www.gospeltractsociety.org
www.thecomingchrist.com

Appendix

Chapter 1 GROUND SCHOOL

1. *And as he sat upon the mount of Olives, the disciples came unto him privately, saying, Tell us, when shall these things be? and what shall be the sign of thy coming, and of the end of the world?* Matthew 24:3

2. *The words of the Lord are pure words: as silver tried in a furnace of earth, purified seven times.* Psalms 12:6

And he said unto them, Go ye into all the world, and preach the gospel to every creature. Mark 16:15

3. *And the dragon was wroth with the woman, and went to make war with the remnant of her seed, which keep the commandments of God, and have the testimony of Jesus Christ.* Revelation 12:17

Chapter 2 THE BIG PICTURE

1. *And I saw a new heaven and a new earth: for the first heaven and the first earth were passed away; and there was no more sea.* Revelation 21:1

2. *And the city had no need of the sun, neither of the moon, to shine in it: for the glory of God did lighten it, and the Lamb is the light thereof.* Revelation 21:3

3. *For since the beginning of the world men have not heard, nor perceived by the ear, neither hath the eye seen, O God, beside thee, what he hath prepared for him that waiteth for him.* Isaiah 64:4;

But as it is written, Eye hath not seen, nor ear heard, neither have entered into the heart of man, the things which God hath prepared for them that love him. I Corinthians 2:9

Chapter 3 THE SEVEN EARTHS

1. "Unlocking the Mysteries of Creation" Dennis R. Petersen, Master Books, Green Forest AR.

2. *And I saw thrones, and they sat upon them, and judgment was given unto them: and I saw the souls of them that were beheaded for the witness of Jesus, and for the word of God, and which had not worshiped the beast, neither his image, neither had received his mark upon their foreheads, or in their hands; and they lived and reigned with Christ a thousand years.* Revelation 20:4

3. *In the midst of the street of it, and on either side of the river, was there the tree of life, which bare twelve manner of fruits, and yielded her fruit every month: and the leaves of the tree were for the healing of the nations.* Revelation 22:2

Chapter 5 WHY ARE WE HERE?

1. *And when the woman saw that the tree was good for food, and that it was pleasant to the eyes, and a tree to be desired to make one wise, she took of the fruit thereof, and did eat, and gave also unto her husband with her; and he did eat.* Genesis 3:6

2. *How art thou fallen from heaven, O Lucifer, son of the morning ! how art thou cut down to the ground, which didst weaken the nations!* Isaiah 14:12

3. *For thou hast said in thine heart, I will ascend into heaven, I will exalt my throne above the stars of God: I will sit also upon the mount of the congregation, in the sides of the north I will ascend above the heights of the clouds; I will be like the most High.* Isaiah 14:13, 14

4. *I form the light, and create darkness: I make peace, and create evil: I the Lord do all these things.* Isaiah 45:7

5. *And the Lord said unto Satan, Behold, all that he hath is in thy power; only upon himself put not forth thine hand. So Satan went forth from the presence of the Lord.* Job 1:12

6. *But of that day and hour knoweth no man, no, not the angels of heaven, but my Father only.* Matthew 24:36

7. *He hath made the earth by his power, he hath established the world by his wisdom, and hath stretched out the heavens by his discretion.* Jeremiah 10:12

8. *For we are his workmanship, created in Christ Jesus unto good works, which God hath before ordained that we should walk in them.* Ephesians 2:10

9. *Thy word is a lamp unto my feet, and a light unto my path.* Psalms 119:105;

In whom we have redemption through his blood, the forgiveness of sins, according to the riches of his grace. Ephesians 1:7

10. *But we are not of them who draw back unto perdition; but of them that believe to the saving of the soul.* Hebrews 10:39

11. *But thou art holy, O thou that inhabits the praises of Israel.* Psalms 22:3

12. *And I saw a new heaven and a new earth: for the first heaven and the first earth were passed away; and there was no more sea.* Revelation 21:1

Chapter 6 THE SCOOP ON SATAN

1. *And he said, I will certainly return unto thee according to the time of life; and, lo, Sarah thy wife shall have a son. And Sarah heard it in the tent door, which was behind him.* Genesis 18:10;

Arise, lift up the lad, and hold him in thine hand; for I will make him a great nation. Genesis 21:18

2. *And many false prophets shall rise, and shall deceive many.* Matthew 24:11

3. www.share-international.org

4. *And it was given unto him to make war with the saints, and to overcome them: and power was given him over all kindreds, and tongues, and nations.* Revelation 13:7

5. *And he shall speak great words against the most High, and shall wear out the saints of the most High, and think to change times and laws: and they shall be given into his hand until a time and times and the dividing of time.* Daniel 7:25

6. *And they worshiped the dragon which gave power unto the beast: and they worshiped the beast, saying, Who is like unto the beast? who is able to make war with him?* Revelation 13:4

7. *And his power shall be mighty, but not by his own power: and he shall destroy wonderfully, and shall prosper, and practise, and shall destroy the mighty and the holy people.* Daniel 8:24;

And after the league made with him he shall work deceitfully: for he shall come up, and shall become strong with a small people. Daniel 11:23

Chapter 7 THE END-TIME PUZZLE: PUTTING IT ALL TOGETHER

1. *Many will say to me in that day, Lord, Lord, have we not prophesied in thy name? and in thy name have cast out devils? and in thy name done many wonderful works? And then will I profess unto them, I never knew you: depart from me, ye that work iniquity.* Matthew 7:22, 23

2. *Let no man decieve you by any means: for that day shall not come, except there come a falling away first, and that man of sin be revealed, the son of perdition:* 2 Thessalonians 2:3

Because thou hast kept the word of my patience, I also will keep thee from the hour of temptation, which shall come upon all the world, to try them that dwell upon the earth. Revelation 3:10

3. *All that the Father giveth me shall come to me; and him that cometh to me I will in no wise cast out.* John 6:37

4. *And he said, Go thy way, Daniel: for the words are closed up and sealed till the time of the end.* Daniel 12:9

5. *Seventy weeks are determined upon thy people and upon thy holy city, to finish the transgression, and to make an end of sins, and to make reconciliation for iniquity, and to bring in everlasting righteousness, and to seal up the vision and prophecy, and to anoint the most Holy.* Daniel 9:24

6. *For godly sorrow worketh repentance to salvation not to be repented of: but the sorrow of the world worketh death.* 2 Corinthians 7:10

Chapter 8 SORTING THE PUZZLE PIECES

1. *And the seventh angel sounded; and there were great voices in heaven, saying, The kingdoms of this world are become the kingdoms of our Lord, and of his Christ; and he shall reign for ever and ever.* Revelation 11:15

Chapter 9 DANIEL IDENTIFIES THREE GROUPS

1. *But tidings out of the east and out of the north shall trouble him: therefore he shall go forth with great fury to destroy, and utterly to take away many. And he shall plant the tabernacles of his palace between the seas in the glorious holy mountain; yet he shall come to his end, and none shall help him.* Daniel 11:44, 45

2. *And they shall see his face; and his name shall be in their foreheads.* Revelation 22:4

3. *Wherefore seeing we also are compassed about with so great a cloud of witnesses, let us lay aside every weight, and the sin which doth so easily beset us, and let us run with patience the race that is set before us.* Hebrews 12:1

4. *And I saw thrones, and they sat upon them, and judgment was given unto them: and I saw the souls of them that were beheaded for the witness of Jesus, and for the word of God, and which had not worshiped the beast, neither his image, neither had received his mark upon their foreheads, or in their hands; and they lived and reigned with Christ a thousand years.* Revelation 20:4

5. *And he shall judge among the nations, and shall rebuke many people: and they shall beat their swords into plowshares, and their spears into pruning hooks: nation shall not lift up sword against nation, neither shall they learn war any more.* Isaiah 2:4;

And he shall judge among many people, and rebuke strong nations afar off; and they shall beat their swords into plowshares, and their spears into pruning hooks: nation shall not lift up a sword against nation, neither shall they learn war any more. Micah 4:3

Chapter 10 THE FIRST AND SECOND RESURRECTIONS

1. *The first of the first fruits of thy land thou shalt bring into the house of the Lord thy God. Thou shalt not seethe a kid in his mother's milk.* Exodus 23:19

2. *And another angel came out from the altar, which had power over fire; and cried with a loud cry to him that had the sharp sickle, saying, Thrust in thy sharp sickle, and gather the clusters of the vine of the earth; for her grapes are fully ripe.* Revelation 14:18;

Be patient therefore, brethren, unto the coming of the Lord. Behold, the husbandman waiteth for the precious fruit of the earth, and hath long patience for it, until he receive the early and latter rain. James 5:7

3. *And I saw a great white throne, and him that sat on it, from whose face the earth and the heaven fled away; and there was found no place for them. And I saw the dead, small and great, stand before God; and the books were opened: and another book was opened, which is the book of life: and the dead were judged out of those things which were written in the books, according to their works. And the sea gave up the dead which were in it; and death and hell delivered up the dead which were in them: and they were judged every man according to their works. And death and hell were cast into the lake of fire. This is the second death. And whosoever was not found written in the book of life was cast into the lake of fire.* Revelation 20:11-15

4. *But now is Christ risen from the dead, and become the first fruits of them that slept.* 1 Corinthians 15:20

5. *And when the thousand years are expired, Satan shall be loosed out of his prison.* Revelation 20:7

6. *And shall go out to deceive the nations which are in the four quarters of the earth, God and Magog, to gather them together to battle: the nubmer of whom is as the sand of the sea. And they went up on the breadth of the earth, and compassed the camp of the saints about, and the beloved city: and fire came down from God out of heaven, and devoured them.* Revelation 20:8, 9

7. *And death and hell were cast into the lake of fire. This is the second death.* Revelation 20:14;

But the fearful, and unbelieving, and the abominable, and murderers, and whoremongers, and sorcerers, and idolaters, and all liars, shall have their part in the lake which burneth with fire and brimstone: which is the second death. Revelation 21:8

Chapter 11 TIMING IS EVERYTHING

1. The Master Plan, Harvest House Publishers, copyright 1993 by Lamb & Lion Ministries, p. 108

2. *Blessed is he that waiteth, and cometh to the thousand three hundred and five and thirty days.* Daniel 12:12

3. *I have trodden the winepress alone; and of the people there was none with me: for I will tread them in mine anger, and trample them in my fury; and their blood shall be sprinkled upon my garments, and I will stain all my raiment. For the day of vengeance is in mine heart, and the year of my redeemed is come.* Isaiah 63:3, 4

4. *Jesus said unto her, I am the resurrection, and the life: he that believeth in me, though he were dead, yet shall he live.* John 11:25

Chapter 12 THE TIME LINE

1. *Behold, your house is left unto you desolate: and verily I say unto you, Ye shall not see me, until the time come when ye shall say, Blessed is he that cometh in the name of the Lord.* Luke 13:35

2. *But of that day and hour knoweth no man, no, not the angels of heaven, but my Father only.* Matthew 24:36;

But of that day and that hour knoweth no man, no, not the angels which are in heaven, neither the Son, but the Father. Mark 13:32

3. *Alas! for that day is great, so that none is like it: it is even the time of Jacob's trouble; but he shall be saved out of it.* Jeremiah 30:7

4. *And I heard the man clothed in linen, which was upon the waters of the river, when he held up his right hand and his left hand unto heaven, and sware by him that liveth for ever that it shal be for a time, times, and an half; and when he shall have accomplished to scatter the power of the holy people, all these things shall be finished.* Daniel 12:17

5. *When ye therefore shall see the abomination of desolation, spoken of by Daniel the prophet, stand in the holy place, (whoso readeth, let him understand)* Matthew 24:15;

And the king shall do according to his will; and he shall exalt himself, and magnify himself above every god and shall speak marvellous things against the God of gods, and shall prosper till the indignation be accomplished: for that that is determined shall be done. Daniel 11:36

6. *And from the time that the daily sacrifice shall be taken away, and the abomination that maketh desolate set up, there shall be a thousand two*

hundred and ninety days. Daniel 12:11

7. *And at that time shall Michael stand up, the great prince which standeth for the children of thy people: and there shall be a time of trouble, such as never was since there was a nation even to that same time: and at that time thy people shall be delivered, every one that shall be found written in the book.* Daniel 12:1;

For then shall be great tribulation, such as was not since the beginning of the world to this time, no, nor ever shall be. Matthew 24:21

8. *And the king shall do according to his will; and he shall exalt himself, and magnify himself above every god, and shall speak marvellous things against the God of gods, and shall prosper till the indignation be accomplished: for that that is determined shall be done.* Daniel 11:36;

When ye therefore shall see the abomination of desolation, spoken of by Daniel the prophet, stand in the holy place, (whoso readeth, let him understand) Matthew 24:15

9. *For when they shall say, Peace and safety; then sudden destruction cometh upon them, as travail upon a woman with child; and they shall not escape.* 1 Thessalonians 5:3

10. *Then let them which are in Judea flee to the mountains; and let them which are in the midst of it depart out; and let not them that are in the countries enter there into.* Luke 21:21

11. *And the dragon was wroth with the woman, and went to make war with the remnant of her seed, which keep the commandments of God, and have the testimony of Jesus Christ.* Revelation 21:17

12. *And he causeth all, both small and great, rich and poor, free and bond, to receive a mark in their right hand, or in their foreheads: And that no man might buy or sell, save he that had the mark, or the name of the beast, or the number of his name.* Revelation 13:16, 17

Chapter 13 THE TIME OF THE GREAT TRIBULATION

1. *And at that time shall Michael stand up, the great prince which standeth for the children of thy people: and there shall be a time of trouble, such as never was since there was a nation even to that same time: and at that time*

thy people shall be delivered, every one that shall be found written in the book. Daniel 12:1

2. *For the word of the Lord is right; and all his works are done in truth.* Psalms 33:4

3. *And the smoke of their torment ascendeth up for ever and ever: and they have no rest day nor night, who worship the beast and his image, and whosoever receiveth the mark of his name.* Revelation 14:11

4. *For when they shall say, Peace and safety; then sudden destruction cometh upon them, as travail upon a woman with child; and they shall not escape.* 1 Thessalonians 5:3

5. *And I saw thrones, and they sat upon them, and judgment was given unto them: and I saw the souls of them that were beheaded for the witness of Jesus, and for the word of God, and which had not worshiped the beast, neither his image, neither had received his mark upon their foreheads, or in their hands; and they lived and reigned with Christ a thousand years.* Revelation 20:4

6. *But tidings out of the east and out of the north shall trouble him: therefore he shall go forth with great fury to destroy, and utterly to take away many.* Daniel 11:44;

After this I beheld, and, lo, a great multitude, which no man could number, of all nations, and kindreds, and people, and tongues, stood before the throne, and before the Lamb, clothed with white robes, and palms in their hands. Revelation 7:9

7. *Then shall they deliver you up to be afflicted, and shall kill you: and ye shall be hated of all nations for my name's sake. And then shall many be offended, and shall betray one another, and shall hate one another.* Matthew 24:9, 10; Luke 21:12, 16, 17

8. *And it was given unto him to make war with the saints, and to overcome them: and power was given him over all kindreds, and tongues, and nations.* Revelation 13: 7

9. *And when the dragon saw that he was cast unto the earth, he persecuted the woman which brought forth the man child.* Revelation 12:13

10. *For thou hast said in thine heart, I will ascend into heaven, I will exalt my throne above the stars of God: I will sit also upon the mount of the con-*

gregation, in the sides of the north: I will ascend above the heights of the clouds; I will be like the most High. Isaiah 14:13, 14

11. *And I saw the woman drunken with the blood of the saints, and with the blood of the martyrs of Jesus: and when I saw her, I wondered with great admiration.* Revelation 17:6

12. *And he shall plant the tabernacle of his palace between the seas in the glorious holy mountain; yet he shall come to his end, and none shall help him.* Daniel 11:45

And the beast was taken and with him the false prophet that wrought miracles before him, with which he deceived them that had received the mark of the beast, and them that worshiped his image. These both were cast alive into a lake of fire burning with brimstone. Revelation 19:20

13. *And he causeth all, both small and great, rich and poor, free and bond, to receive a mark in their right hand, or in their foreheads: And that no man might buy or sell, save he that had the mark, or the name of the beast, or the number of his name.* Revelation 13:16, 17

14. *And he shall speak great words against the most High, and shall wear out the saints of the most High, and think to change times and laws: and they shall be given into his hand until a time and times and the dividing of time.* Daniel 7:25

15. *But before all these, they shall lay their hands on you, and persecute you, delivering you up to the synagogues, and into prisons, being brought before kings and rulers for my name's sake.* Luke 21:12

16. *And through his policy also he shall cause craft to prosper in his hand; and he shall magnify himself in his heart, and by peace shall destroy many: he shall also stand up against the Prince of princes; but he shall be broken without hand.* Daniel 8:25

17. *And it was given unto him to make war with the saints, and to overcome them: and power was given to him over all kindreds, and tongues, and nations.* Revelation 13:17

18. *And when the dragon saw that he was cast unto the earth, he persecuted the woman which brought forth the man child.* Revelation 12:13

19. *And the beast was taken and with him the false prophet that wrought miracles before him, with which he deceived them that had received the*

mark of the beast, and them that worshiped his image. These both were cast alive into a lake of fire burning with brimstone. Revelation 19:20

20. *And he shall speak great words against the most High, and shall wear out the saints of the most High, and think to change times and laws: and they shall be given into his hand until a time and times and the dividing of time.* Daniel 7:25

21. *He shall enter peaceably even upon the fattest places of the province; and he shall do that which his fathers have not done, nor his fathers' fathers; he shall scatter among them the prey, and spoil, and riches: yea, and he shall forecast his devices against the strong holds, even for a time.* Daniel 11:24

22. *Who opposeth and exalteth himself above all that is called God, or that is worshiped; so that he as God sitteth in the temple of God, shewing himself that he is God.* 2 Thessalonians 2:4

23. *And he shall speak great words against the most High, and shall wear out the saints of the most High, and think to change times and laws: and they shall be given into his hand until a time and times and the dividing of time.* Daniel 7:25

24. *And all that dwell upon the earth shall worship him, whose names are not written in the book of life of the Lamb slain from the foundation of the world.* Revelation 13:8

25. *And the beast was taken, and with him the false prophet that wrought miracles before him, with which he deceived them that had received the mark of the beast, and them that worshiped his image. These both were cast alive into a lake of fire burning with brimstone.* Revelation 19:20

26. *Even him, whose coming is after the working of Satan with all power and signs and lying wonders.* 2 Thessalonians 2:9

27. *And it was given unto him to make war with the saints, and to overcome them: and power was given him over all kindreds, and tongues, and nations.* Revelation 13:7

28. *And in the latter time of their kingdom, when the transgressors are come to the full, a king of fierce countenance, and understanding dark sentences, shall stand up. And his power shall be mighty, but not by his own power: and he shall destroy wonderfully, and shall prosper, and practise, and shall destroy the mighty and the holy people.* Daniel 8:23, 24

29. A shrine located on the Temple Mount in the Old City of Jerusalem. www.wikipedia.org

Chapter 14 HOW TO KNOW THE ANTICHRIST

1. *And the ten horns out of this kingdom are ten kings that shall arise: and another shall rise after them; and he shall be diverse from the first, and he shall subdue three kings.* Daniel 7:24

2. *And I saw one of his heads as it were wounded to death; and his deadly wound was healed: and all the world wondered after the beast.* Revelation 13:3

3. *And deceiveth them that dwell on the earth by the means of those miracles which he had power to do in the sight of the beast; saying to them that dwell on the earth, that they should make an image to the beast, which had the wound by a sword, and did live.* Revelation 13:14

4. *And they worshiped the dragon which gave power unto the beast: and they worshipped the beast, saying, Who is like unto the beast? who is able to make war with him?* Revelation 13:4

5. *Then if any man shall say unto you, Lo, here is Christ, or there; believe it not. For there shall arise false Christs, and false prophets, and shall shew great signs and wonders; insomuch that, if it were possible, they shall deceive the very elect.* Matthew 24:23, 24

6. *Behold, he cometh with clouds; and every eye shall see him, and they also which pierced him: and all kindreds of the earth shall wail because of him. Even so, Amen.* Revelation 1:7

7. *And all that dwell upon the earth shall worship him, whose names are not written in the book of life of the Lamb slain from the foundation of the world.* Revelation 13:8

8. *And the beast was taken, and with him the false prophet that wrought miracles before him, with which he deceived them that had received the mark of the beast, and them that worshiped his image. These both were cast alive into a lake of fire burning with brimstone. And the remnant were slain with the sword of him that sat upon the horse, which sword proceeded out of his mouth: and all the fowls were filled with their flesh.* Revelation 19: 20, 21

9. *They shall put you out of the synagogues: yea, the time cometh, that whosoever killeth you will think that he doeth God service.* John 16:2

10. *And then shall appear the sign of the Son of man in heaven: and then shall all the tribes of the earth mourn, and they shall see the Son of man coming in the clouds of heaven with power and great glory.* Matthew 24:30

11. *Here is wisdom. Let him that hath understanding count the number of the beast: for it is the number of a man; and his number is Six hundred threescore and six.* Revelation 13:18

12. *And he had power to give life unto the image of the beast, that the image of the beast should both speak, and cause that as many as would not worship the image of the beast should be killed.* Revelation 13:15

13. *And he causeth all, both small and great, rich and poor, free and bond, to receive a mark in their right hand, or in their foreheads.* Revelation 13:16

Chapter 15 HOW CAN CHRISTIANS PREPARE FOR THE GREAT TRIBULATION?

1. *But when they shall lead you, and deliver you up, take no thought beforehand what ye shall speak, neither do ye premeditate: but whatsoever shall be given you in that hour, that speak ye: for it is not ye that speak, but the Holy Ghost.* Mark 13:11; Luke 21:14, 15

2. *For God sent not his Son into the world to condemn the world; but that the world through him might be saved. He that believeth on him is not condemned: but he that believeth not is condemned already, because he hath not believed in the name of the only begotten Son of God.* John 3:17,18

Chapter 17 THE DARK DAYS OF THE GREAT TRIBULATION

1. *And this gospel of the kingdom shall be preached in all the world for a witness unto all nations; and then shall the end come.* Matthew 24:14

2. *And I will give power unto my two witnesses, and they shall prophesy a thousand two hundred and threescore days, clothed in sackcloth.* Revelation 11:3

3. *And as it is appointed unto men once to die, but after this the judgment.* Hebrews 9:27

4. *And the nations were angry, and thy wrath is come, and the time of the dead, that they should be judged, and that thou shouldest give reward unto thy servants the prophets, and to the saints, and them that fear thy name, small and great; and shouldest destroy them which destroy the earth.* Revelation 11:18

5. *And I saw heaven opened, and behold a white horse; and he that sat upon him was called Faithful and True, and in righteousness he doth judge and make war. His eyes were as a flame of fire, and on his head were many crowns; and he had a name written, that no man knew, but he himself. And he was clothed with a vesture dipped in blood: and his name is called The Word of God.* Revelation 19:11-13

6. *And said to the mountains and rocks, Fall on us, and hide us from the face of him that sitteth on the throne, and from the wrath of the Lamb.* Revelation 6:16; 9:6

7. *Who shall be punished with everlasting destruction from the presence of the Lord, and from the glory of his power.* 2 Thessalonians 1:9

Chapter 18 THE SECOND COMING OF CHRIST-THE DAY OF JUDGMENT

1. *Looking for and hasting unto the coming of the day of God, wherein the heavens being on fire shall be dissolved, and the elements shall melt with fervent heat.* 2 Peter 3:12

2. *For yourselves know perfectly that the day of the Lord so cometh as a thief in the night. For when they shall say, Peace and safety; then sudden destruction cometh upon them, as travail upon a woman with child; and they shall not escape. But ye, brethren, are not in darkness, that that day should overtake you as a thief. Ye are all the children of light, and the children of the day: we are not of the night, nor of darkness.* 1 Thessalonians 5:2-5

3. *Looking for that blessed hope, and the glorious appearing of the great God and our Saviour Jesus Christ.* Titus 2:13

4. *For the Lord himself shall descend from heaven with a shout, with the voice of the archangel, and with the trump of God: and the dead in Christ*

shall rise first. Then we which are alive and remain shall be caught up together with them in the clouds, to meet the Lord in the air: and so shall we ever be with the Lord. 1 Thessalonians 4:16, 17

5. And many of them that sleep in the dust of the earth shall awake, some to everlasting life, and some to shame and everlasting contempt. Daniel 12:2

6. For as the lightning cometh out of the east, and shineth even unto the west; so shall also the coming of the Son of man be. Matthew 24:27

7. And when he had opened the seventh seal, there was silence in heaven about the space of half an hour. Revelation 8:1

8. And the nations were angry, and thy wrath is come, and the time of the dead, that they should be judged, and that thou shouldest give reward unto thy servants the prophets, and to the saints, and them that fear thy name, small and great; and shouldest destroy them which destroy the earth. Revelation 11:18

Chapter 19 GOD'S WRATH AND THE AFTERMATH

1. And from the time that the daily sacrifice shall be taken away, and the abomination that maketh desolate set up, there shall be a thousand two hundred and ninety days. Blessed is he that waiteth, and cometh to the thousand three hundred and five and thirty days. Daniel 12:11, 12

2. And I saw an angel standing in the sun; and he cried with a loud voice, saying to all the fowls that fly in the midst of heaven, Come and gather yourselves together unto the supper of the great God; That ye may eat the flesh of kings, and the flesh of captains, and the flesh of mighty men, and the flesh of horses, and of them that sit on them, and the flesh of all men, both free and bond, both small and great. Revelation 19:17, 18

Chapter 20 THE "WHY" OF IT

1. And I saw a new heaven and a new earth: for the first heaven and the first earth were passed away; and there was no more sea. And I John saw the holy city, new Jerusalem, coming down from God out of heaven, prepared as a bride adorned for her husband. Revelation 21:1, 2

2. But, beloved, be not ignorant of this one thing, that one day is with the Lord as a thousand years, and a thousand years as one day. 2 Peter 3:8

3. *It came to pass after this also, that the children of Moab, and the children of Ammon, and with them other beside the Ammonites, came against Jehoshaphat to battle.* 2 Chronicles 20:1

4. *And shall go out to deceive tha nations which are in the four quarters of the earth, God and Magog, to gather them together to battle: the number of whom is as the sand of the sea. And they went up on the breadth of the earth, and compassed the camp of the saints about, and the beloved city: and fire came down from God out of heaven, and devoured them.* Revelation 20:8, 9

5. *The wolf and the lamb shall feed together, and the lion shall eat straw like the bullock: and dust shall be the serpent's meat. They shall not hurt nor destroy in all my holy mountain, saith the Lord.* Isaiah 65:25

6. *And he shall judge among the nations, and shall rebuke many people: and they shall beat their swords into plowshares, and their spears into pruning hooks: nation shall not lift up sword against nation, neither shall they learn war any more.* Isaiah 2:4; Micah 4:3

7. *And I saw thrones, and they sat upon them, and judgment was given unto them: and I saw the souls of them that were beheaded for the witness of Jesus, and for the word of God, and which had not worshiped the beast, neither his image, neither had received his mark upon their foreheads, or in their hands; and they lived and reigned with Christ a thousand years.* Revelation 20:4

8. *These shall make war with the Lamb, and the Lamb shall overcome them: for he is Lord of lords, and King of kings: and they that are with him are called, and chosen, and faithful.* Revelation 17:14

9. *Nevertheless the people refused to obey the voice of Samuel; and they said , Nay; but we will have a king over us; That we also may be like all the nations; and that our king may judge us, and go out before us, and fight our battles. And Samuel heard all the words of the people, and he rehearsed them in the ears of the Lord. And the Lord said to Samuel, Hearken unto their voice, and make them a king. And Samuel said unto the men of Israel, Go ye every man unto his city.* 1 Samuel 8:19-22

10. *And hast made us unto our God kings and priests: and we shall reign on the earth.* Revelation 5:10

11. *In a moment, in the twinkling of an eye, at the last trump: for the trumpet shall sound, and the dead shall be raised incorruptible, and we shall be changed.* 1 Corinthians 15:52

12. *But the rest of the dead lived not again until the thousand years were finished. This is the first resurrection.* Revelation 20:5

13. *And the city lieth foursquare, and the length is as large as the breadth: and he measured the city with the reed, twelve thousand furlongs. The length and the breadth and the height of it are equal.* Revelation 21:16

14. *That I may know him, and the power of his resurrection, and the fellowship of his sufferings, being made conformable unto his death.* Philippians 3:10

About the Author:

Tom Buttram has served as Director of Missions for the out-reach to Haiti, begun by his father in 1964. Since his calling in '82, Tom has made over 140 trips to lead pastor conferences, establish churches, schools and an orphanage. At home, he has taught college level Sunday School classes for 23 years, and twice served churches as interim pastor. He has written articles of faith for the "Gospel Tract Harvester" for 30 years and since 2006, served as President of the Gospel Tract Society. His love for nature, farming, flying and mechanics—have enabled him to relay the logic of the Gospel to the unbelieving and helped many see the nature of God, in the nature of His Creation. Married to Shirley since 1969, they have two children, Justin and Emily, and five grandchildren, to whom this book is dedicated.